W9-AQT-096

Protecting Intellectual Property Rights

Protecting Intellectual Property Rights

Issues and Controversies

Robert P. Benko

American Enterprise Institute for Public Policy Research

Washington, D.C.

Robert P. Benko is a research associate with the Competing in a Changing World Economy project at the American Enterprise Institute.

Distributed by arrangement with

UPA, Inc.
4720 Boston Way
Lanham, MD 20706
3 Henrietta Street
London WC2E 8LU England

Library of Congress Cataloging-in-Publication Data

Benko, Robert P.
  Protecting intellectual property rights.

  (AEI studies ; 453)
  Bibliography: p.
  1. Intellectual property—United States.
2. Intellectual property (International law) I. Title.
II. Series.
KF2979.B36   1987   346.7304'8   86-32124
ISBN 0-8447-3617-1 (alk. paper)   347.30648
ISBN 0-8447-3622-8 (pbk. : alk. paper)

1   3   5   7   9   10   8   6   4   2

AEI Studies 453

Printed in the United States of America

Contents

Foreword

For many decades the United States has enjoyed great economic success in international markets. In recent years, however, the competitiveness of many American goods and services has diminished. Current U.S. trade woes have forced policy makers to reassess the bases of our competitive strength to determine where the problems lie and how they might be corrected.

Numerous studies of American competitiveness, including the President's Commission on Industrial Competitiveness, have emphasized that the chief competitive advantage of the United States lies in its technological superiority. Prominent among the issues designated as crucial to our continued technological and competitive standing is the international protection of intellectual property rights— copyrights, patents, and trademarks. Creating new technologies is costly, time consuming, and risky. Investors cannot assume these costs and risks without assurance that, if their efforts produce a viable new technology, they will have sufficient control over that technology to earn a return on their investment. Intellectual property rights provide that assurance. They establish the economic incentives for creative activity, research, development, and technological innovation.

In many cases, however, the international protection of intellectual property rights is uncertain or nonexistent. American businesses complain increasingly about the unauthorized foreign acquisition and exploitation of intellectual properties and the heavy losses imposed on the U.S. economy. The violation of intellectual property rights causes immediate economic hardships and undermines incentives for future innovations. As a result, our most important competitive asset is damaged and with it our ability to compete worldwide.

For this reason, policy makers responsible for American trade policy have become increasingly concerned with intellectual property issues. Yet much confusion still exists over the details of intellectual property law and enforcement in international markets. Few international trade experts have worked extensively in this complicated and often confusing field.

Robert Benko's introductory monograph on emerging trade-related intellectual property issues is designed to clear up some of this confusion. The monograph provides essential definitions, a review of the existing legal regime, an introduction to the history and economics of intellectual property rights, and a summary of the major policy issues. It also offers some suggestions for additional research.

Although important intellectual property negotiations have already begun, most notably in the General Agreement on Tariffs and Trade (GATT), many issues remain unresolved. More data, research, and study must be pursued before we can expect to resolve them adequately, particularly in the area of new technologies such as semiconductor chips, computer software, and biotechnology.

Benko's monograph is one of a series of conferences, seminars, publications, and special events of the American Enterprise Institute's multiyear research project "Competing in a Changing World Economy." This project examines structural changes in the world economy and explores strategies for dealing with new economic, political, and strategic realities facing the United States.

CHRISTOPHER C. DeMUTH
President
American Enterprise Institute

1
Introduction

Until recently the international protection of intellectual property rights was of concern only to a few lawyers trained in the complex legal technicalities dominating the field. The challenge to the competitive standing of the United States in the international economy over the past decade, however, has elevated these once obscure issues to the top of the economic and trade policy agendas. Declining U.S. economic and trade fortunes have prompted reevaluation of the many factors underlying the competitiveness of American goods and services. Much study has focused specifically on U.S. technological capabilities, in recognition that our competitive advantage rests largely on our technological superiority. Concern for the protection of intellectual property rights is just one dimension of the larger concern over our capacity to innovate and ultimately to compete in the increasingly competitive world marketplace.

Interest and activity in the intellectual property area have emerged and continue to grow in the federal government, Congress, business organizations, and research and academic circles. The report of the President's Commission on Industrial Competitiveness in January 1985 urged that the "strengthening of intellectual property rights at home and abroad should be a priority item on the nation's policy agenda."[1] Following the commission's advice, President Ronald Reagan made intellectual property rights a priority in a trade statement on September 23, 1985.[2] The Office of the U.S. Trade Representative, the Department of Commerce, and the Department of State have since taken the lead in the administration on these issues, most recently announcing a multifaceted program including domestic legislation and trade strategies designed to improve the protection of intellectual property.

Congressional interest has also been strong. The Ninety-eighth Congress passed a number of intellectual property measures, including two important trade-related acts—the Trade and Tariff Act of 1984 and the Caribbean Basin Economic Recovery Act. Pending legislative proposals cover an even broader range of intellectual property issues.

1

Finally, the real leadership on intellectual property has come from the private business sector in the United States. The U.S. Council for International Business, the Association of Data Processing Service Organizations, the Coalition of Service Industries, the Motion Picture Export Association of America, the American Electronics Association, and many others have focused their substantial energies and influence on improving the protection of intellectual property rights at home and abroad.

Despite all this activity, considerable confusion still surrounds the intellectual property issue. A growing consensus supports the view that world intellectual property rights need to be strengthened. But just what that view entails and how it should be promoted are questions still open to debate. Much confusion stems from the extremely diverse and complex issues that fall into the category of the protection of intellectual property rights.

This book is designed as an introduction to these issues and to the debates now taking place on public policy. It seeks to identify the full range of relevant issues and to clarify some of the surrounding debate. It was also created to serve as a resource for those well versed in one or more of the specific issues by collecting a broad range of information and in the hope of stimulating additional research into those issues, which are of fundamental importance to the competitive health and well-being of the United States.

Definitions

Intellectual property can be divided into two main classifications—industrial property and copyrights.

Industrial Property. Industrial property includes inventions, trademarks, and industrial designs. These terms have no universally accepted definitions. Definitions vary from country to country, but the following are widely accepted:

- *Inventions* are novel ideas that permit in practice the solution of specific technological problems. They may be protected by patents or by trade secrets. Patents legally protect the idea, usually granting the patentee exclusive rights over the exploitation of the invention. To be patentable, an idea is required by most countries to be new, non-obvious, and immediately applicable to industry. The criteria necessary to satisfy each of these requirements vary from country to country. Protection is usually granted for fifteen to twenty years, although notable exceptions exist. Trade secrets also protect the idea but rely exclusively on private measures, not public law or guarantees, to prevent disclosure.

• *Trademarks* are marks to distinguish goods or services of an industrial or commercial enterprise or group of enterprises. They include words, letters, numbers, drawings, pictures, emblems, monograms, signatures, colors, and occasionally packaging forms. Most countries require registration of the mark for protection. Usually there are no time limits on trademark protection, although many countries require periodic reregistration.

• *Industrial designs* are ornamental aspects of a useful article, such as shape, lines, or color. The design must not be dictated by the function of the article. Normally designs must be proved original or novel and must be registered for protection, which is usually granted for fifteen to twenty years.

Copyrights. Works that may be copyrighted include literary, musical, artistic, photographic, and cinematographic works, maps, and technical drawings. Many copyright laws also cover works of applied art such as jewelry and furniture, choreographic works, records, tapes, and broadcasts. Copyrights do not protect ideas but only the expression of ideas. Protection covers the use of a work. To be copyrightable, the work need only be original or not a copy; it need not be novel. Many countries grant copyright protection automatically. Others require compliance with certain formalities, such as registration, registration fees, or copyright notices on published copies. Copyright duration generally extends fifty years beyond the life of the author. Numerous exceptions exist, however, depending on the kind of work and the particular use.

Notes

1. President's Commission on Industrial Competitiveness, *Global Competition, the New Reality* (Washington, D.C., 1985), p. 52.

2. "The President Announces New Trade Policy," *Business America*, September 30, 1985, p. 2.

2
International Agreements and Domestic Law

International Agreements

The international regime for the protection of intellectual property rights is naturally one focus of concern in current policy debates. The term "international regime" is somewhat misleading. International, regional, and bilateral agreements covering intellectual property issues are governed by an institutionally fragmented network of organizations. No international provisions or bodies are designed to enforce intellectual property rights or to settle disputes. The agreements vary widely in number of participants and therefore in effect. They also suffer from substantive problems.

Most international agreements designed explicitly to protect intellectual property fall under the jurisdiction of the World Intellectual Property Organization (WIPO), but that jurisdiction is by no means all-inclusive. Many other treaties and agreements, covering areas from satellites to maritime trade, contain provisions for the protection of intellectual property rights.

World Intellectual Property Organization. The World Intellectual Property Organization was created by the WIPO convention on July 14, 1967, came into force in 1970, and was made a specialized agency of the United Nations (UN) in December 1974.[1] WIPO has two main objectives: to promote the protection of intellectual property rights by encouraging new treaties and the modernization of domestic laws and by collecting and providing information and technical assistance; and to ensure cooperation among intellectual property unions by centralizing their administration. Membership is open to any state that is a member of the Paris or the Berne union and to any other state that is a member of the UN, any specialized agency of the UN, or the International Atomic Energy Agency, is a party to the statute

4

of the International Court of Justice, or is invited by the general assembly of WIPO. The current membership is 101 states.

Industrial Property Agreements. No international laws stipulate explicit rules for the protection of industrial property. Industrial property laws are specific to each country and cover only acts accomplished or committed in that country. International industrial property treaties or agreements generally do not establish rights but are designed principally to harmonize divergent national laws. Such agreements have been concluded mainly under the Paris Union, established by the Paris Convention in 1883. Twelve such agreements exist and are governed by WIPO.

The Paris Convention is the principal international agreement governing industrial property. It covers such property in the widest sense—inventions, trade names, trademarks, service marks, industrial designs, utility models, indications of source, and appellations of origin. The convention established the core principles of the international patent regime. It provides for national treatment, which requires each contracting state to grant the same protection to nationals of other contracting states as it grants to its own nationals. It also establishes rights of priority; these stipulate that once an application for protection is filed in one country belonging to the agreement, the applicant has twelve months to file in any other contracting state, which then must regard such an application as if it were filed on the same day as the original application.

The United States does not belong to numerous industrial property agreements, generally for one of three reasons: the agreement violates existing U.S. law; U.S. law is stronger; or the agreement is not in the interests of the United States. For example, the Lisbon Agreement might endanger U.S. wine exports because of French claims that the use of terms like "burgundy" and "champagne" violates appellations of origin. A brief summary of the Paris Convention and other major international industrial property agreements can be found in the appendix of this paper.

Copyright Agreements. Again, no international laws specify explicit rules for worldwide copyright protection. Protection is based on national laws effective only in a particular country.

The oldest and most comprehensive international copyright agreement is the Berne Convention, in effect since 1886. WIPO administers the convention, which covers the protection of literary and artistic works in the widest sense. It establishes the principle of national treatment and provides for protection without formalities, for the independence of protection, and for certain minimum rights.

The other major international copyright agreement is the Universal Copyright Convention (UCC), established in 1952 and administered by the UN Educational, Scientific, and Cultural Organization (UNESCO). It provides for many of the principles found in the Berne Convention, including national treatment, with some notable exceptions. A brief summary of these and other international copyright agreements can be found in the appendix.

The U.S. record on international copyright accords is less than exemplary. Until 1891 the United States did not recognize any foreign copyright. The Chace International Copyright Act of 1891 established a framework for bilateral copyright agreements based on reciprocity, but the United States refused to join an international copyright convention until it joined the UCC in 1952.

A longstanding point of international contention has been U.S. refusal to join the premier instrument of international copyright, the Berne Convention. The U.S. decision not to participate was motivated by a wish to preserve certain formalities, including registration requirements, and to preserve such protectionist measures as the requirement of manufacture in the United States.

American accession to the Berne Convention was further complicated in 1928 when the Rome text added the concept of "moral rights." Anglo-American copyright law focuses on economic and property rights. Continental law adds to these author's rights, or moral rights, which further recognize the author's interest in the "personality" of the work. Moral rights do not pass with the sale of the copyright. Authors may still protect against editorial distortion and the like. In the United States protection of this sort can generally be established only by contracts and agreements, although California, New York, and Massachusetts have recently passed moral rights laws. The addition of the moral rights clause to the Berne Convention created a barrier that continues to interfere with U.S. accession to the agreement.

U.S. failure to join Berne has caused ill feeling among many other nations. The United States has been able to enjoy protection without offering reciprocal rights to members. U.S. authors obtain Berne rights through the back door by publishing first or simultaneously in a Berne member country such as Canada. Protection is also achieved through the side door: the national treatment provisions of the UCC ensure Berne protection in all countries that are joint Berne-UCC signatories (fifty-two states). Other nations justifiably argue that the United States cannot simultaneously advocate the principles of international copyright protection and ignore the responsibilities of the Berne.

Support for Berne accession by the United States continues to grow, but formidable obstacles remain. These include the moral rights principles and the so-called manufacturing clause. Part of the Copyright Act of 1976, the clause prohibits the import of literary materials in English, written by U.S. citizens or persons domiciled in the United States, and containing U.S. copyrighted materials unless manufactured in the United States or Canada. These and a host of technical problems stand in the way of easy U.S. accession to the Berne Convention.

U.S. Domestic Law

U.S. intellectual property law is based on Article I, section 8, clause 8, of the Constitution, which gives Congress the power to "promote the progress of science and useful arts, by securing for limited times to authors and inventors the exclusive rights to their respective writings and discoveries." The first U.S. copyright law was enacted in 1790, and major revisions were passed in 1831, 1870, and 1909. The law remained little changed until enactment of the 1976 Copyright Act.

U.S. copyright law protects individual works of authorship fixed in any tangible medium of expression. It grants the author exclusive rights to the sale or reproduction of the work, with some important exceptions for such things as fair use. Copyright protection is for the life of the author plus fifty years.

The first U.S. patent law was also enacted in 1790. It too has undergone repeated alteration, most recently in the Ninety-ninth Congress. The law requires an invention to be novel, nonobvious, and useful to receive patent protection, which lasts for seventeen years. The United States also follows the so-called first-to-invent rule. An invention is eligible for protection unless it has been patented or described in the United States or abroad, is in public use, or has been on sale in this country more than one year before the patent application.

Other major U.S. intellectual property laws include the Lanham Act, which provides for trademark protection. Most states also protect proprietors from piracy of trade secrets; they usually require a proprietor to prove that it has made an effort to maintain confidentiality. Section 337 of the Tariff Act of 1930 and section 301 of the Trade Act of 1974 permit the president to take action against violators of intellectual property rights. A summary of these sections can be found in the appendix.

Note

1. World Intellectual Property Organization, *General Information* (Geneva, 1984), p. 5.

3
Recent and Pending Developments

International Developments

World Intellectual Property Organization. In 1981 the Group of 77, along with Australia, Canada, New Zealand, Portugal, Spain, and Turkey, proposed a number of amendments to the patent and trademark agreements administered by WIPO and also suggested that a number of studies of intellectual property rights be undertaken. The group argued that trademarks on pharmaceuticals give firms monopoly rights that are used to raise prices and profits and that the international community gains nothing in return. It urged serious consideration of limiting or prohibiting the use of trademarks for pharmaceuticals, particularly in the developing countries.[1]

The group also proposed that patent agreements be amended to provide for automatic granting of compulsory licenses after thirty months of nonmanufacture or nonproduction by the patent holder, to permit compulsory licenses that give the licensee exclusive rights to use the patent in a country while the original patentee is denied use for up to two and one-half years, and to provide for forfeiture of a patent after five years of not working it in a country. All these proposals are pending in WIPO. Some developing countries threaten that, if the recommended amendments are not adopted, they will use their right to legislate as they wish on internal industrial property matters not covered in the Paris Convention to impose exclusive, nonvoluntary licensing.

Code on Technology Transfer. In 1974 the Group of 77 submitted to the United Nations Conference on Trade and Development (UNCTAD) proposed rules to govern technology transfers.[2] By late 1982, in the latest draft revision of the code, a compromise had been reached on all but a few of the proposed rules. If passed, the code will most likely be in the form of a set of guidelines—not legally binding.

The code covers the assignment, sale, and licensing of most forms of industrial property; the provision of technical skill and expertise

9

in the forms of plans, models, and instructions involving technical and managerial personnel and personnel training; the technical knowledge necessary for the installation and functioning of plant and equipment and turnkey projects; and technical contents of industrial and technical cooperation agreements. Affiliates or subsidiaries located in the recipient country are not covered, although some issues on this point remain outstanding.

The heart of the code concerns restrictions on practices that have been employed in the past in connection with technology transfers. Twenty restrictions are listed, the first fourteen of which seem acceptable to all. The other six lack the support of the developed nations. They deal with limits on the volume or scope of production, the use of quality controls, the obligation to use trademarks, the requirement to provide equity capital or participation in management, the unduly long duration of arrangements, and limits on the use of technology already imported.

GATT Agreement on Measures to Discourage the Importation of Counterfeit Goods. The United States first proposed the adoption of an anticounterfeiting code in the General Agreement on Tariffs and Trade (GATT) in 1978 at the end of the Tokyo round. By late 1979 the United States and the European Community had agreed on a text; Japan and Canada joined in the agreement in 1982. At the GATT ministerial meetings in November 1982, the GATT Secretariat was instructed to prepare a report on the counterfeiting issue. The issue is pending, awaiting the new trade round.

The agreement would require all signatories actively to discourage trade in counterfeit goods. It would establish public sector channels to handle counterfeiting complaints and would provide an international means of enforcement with avenues for consultation and settlement of disputes.

The code would substantially raise the economic risks taken by counterfeiters and would thereby discourage their operations. It would not, however, prevent the sale of counterfeit goods once they cleared customs and would have no bearing on domestically produced counterfeit goods. Major opposition comes from the developing nations and a few of the advanced nations, which argue that counterfeiting issues should be left to WIPO.

UNESCO. Late in 1983 the United States announced that it was pulling out of UNESCO. It argued that UNESCO had become intolerably politicized and excessively hostile to the United States and further criticized the agency for excessive and careless spending. At the end of 1984 the United States withdrew from the agency, costing UNESCO one-fourth of its budget. Since UNESCO administers the UCC, American withdrawal complicates U.S. relations with the administrative and policy apparatus of the UCC.

U.S. Legislative Developments

The Ninety-eighth Congress passed a number of important measures governing the protection of intellectual property rights, and new proposals are pending in the Ninety-ninth Congress. Legislation completed in the Ninety-eighth Congress includes the following.

The Trade and Tariff Act of 1984. This act amended section 301 of the Trade Act of 1974 to clarify the president's authority to impose import restrictions to counter "unjustifiable, unreasonable or discriminatory" acts, policies, or practices, including those that deny fair and equitable "provision of adequate and effective protection of intellectual property rights." "Unjustifiable" was expanded to include any action that denies protection of intellectual property rights. The act also made the protection of U.S. trademarks, patents, and copyrights a goal of U.S. trade negotiating strategy. Finally, the act included provisions for renewal of the general system of preferences (GSP), which require that intellectual property protection be considered before GSP status and privileges are awarded.

The Caribbean Basin Economic Recovery Act. This act requires the president to consider how far copyrights and rights in intellectual property are protected in a country before designating it a "beneficiary country" eligible for tariff preferences. Countries that permit broadcasts without consent of material belonging to a U.S. copyright owner are also ineligible for special preferences, although the president may waive this clause.

The Trademark Counterfeiting Act of 1984. This act amends the Lanham Act to authorize a court to issue an order for the seizure of goods, counterfeit marks, and means of making such marks and to award treble profits or damages and attorney's fees to a prevailing plaintiff when international counterfeiting is found. The act made it a federal crime knowingly and intentionally to traffic in goods and services using a counterfeit trademark.

The Drug Price Competition and Patent Term Restoration Act of 1984. This act authorizes a manufacturer of a post-1962 generic drug

11

to file an abbreviated application with the Food and Drug Administration for approval and requires manufacturers to show that the drug is the same or therapeutically equivalent to the patented drug that it copies. It permits the manufacturer of the generic drug to begin manufacture before the expiration date of the patented drug if the manufacturer can show that the patent is invalid or that the patent would not be infringed. The generic application becomes valid when the patent expires. Finally, the act restores the term of a patent on a product for half the period of regulatory review, not to exceed five years.

The Semiconductor Chip Protection Act of 1984. This act adopts a sui generis approach to semiconductor chip protection. It grants the creator of a mask work exclusive rights—similar to those provided by copyright—to control the reproduction, importation, distribution, and sale of the work. A mask work is defined as a series of related images embodying the pattern of the surface of the layers of a semiconductor chip. Protection lasts for ten years. To be eligible, the mask work need only be original. The act provides civil penalties for violations with fines up to $250,000. Finally, it permits reverse engineering for evaluation, analysis, and teaching purposes and calls for reciprocity.

The Patent Law Amendments Act of 1984. This act prohibits the supplying of components of a patented U.S. invention for assembly abroad. Any such act is liable as patent infringement. The law also establishes a system of statutory invention registration, or defensive patents. The law further prohibits information commonly owned by a company from being used by any individual party in that company as evidence of "prior art" to block a patent application. Only publicly known information may be used to show that an invention is obvious, given the existing state of knowledge, and therefore ineligible for patent protection. This provision was designed to encourage communication among members of research teams. Finally, the act changes the requirements for joint inventors to obtain patent protection and prohibits the importation of products made abroad with a U.S. patented process.

Pending Proposals. Congress is considering a number of intellectual property proposals. These include measures to amend section 337 of the Tariff Act of 1930 to make it easier to stop the importation of counterfeit goods, to extend the patents that protect a production process to cover the final product, to correct loopholes in the process patent law that permit offshore assembly and reimportation of process

12

patented goods, to ease the antitrust restrictions on companies that work together to license new technologies abroad, and to extend the patent term for chemicals and animal drugs. Congress is also considering the question of U.S. accession to the Berne Convention and the future status of the controversial manufacturing clause. Other proposals in the intellectual property area will certainly continue to appear on the legislative agenda.

Recent U.S. Administration Initiatives

Beginning with President Reagan's September 23, 1985, trade speech, the administration considerably stepped up its efforts to strengthen intellectual property protection. In April 1986 the administration announced a plan involving trade negotiations, legislative proposals, and other measures to rectify lapses in intellectual property rights.[3] The cornerstone of this program, which will be implemented jointly by the Departments of Commerce and State and the Office of the U.S. Trade Representative, is a negotiating plan for a proposed intellectual property code in the GATT. The administration plan also contains a broad-based legislative package and a commitment to pursue accession to the Berne Convention.

The White House initiated proceedings against Korea under the expanded section 301 of the 1974 Trade Act. The action prompted an investigation into Korean intellectual property laws and a threat of retaliation unless problems are rectified. Negotiations have already produced improvements in Korean copyright law. Ambassador Clayton Yeutter stresses that similar actions will be taken against other countries that are lax in protecting intellectual property. The administration is also reviewing the records on intellectual property protection of countries eligible for GSP and preferential tariff privileges under the Caribbean Basin Initiative. Violating countries may lose their preferential status.

The administration will also employ bilateral negotiations to improve protection. Asia and South America have been the principal targets of these efforts, successes being scored in such problem areas as Singapore, Hong Kong, and Malaysia. Bilateral efforts include educational and technical assistance programs offered by the Departments of State and Commerce.

Notes

1. Harry Schwartz, "The UN System's War on the Drug Industry," *Regulation* (July/August 1982), p. 21.

2. Dennis Thompson, "The UNCTAD Code on Transfer of Technology," *Journal of World Trade Law*, vol. 16 (July/August 1982), pp. 311–37.

3. Art Pine, "White House Seeks to Boost Protection for Patents, Copyrights, Trademarks," *Wall Street Journal*, April 8, 1986, p. 7.

4
Economic Theory and Intellectual Property Rights

"Intellectual property rights—patents, trademarks, tradedress, copyrights, trade secrets," notes the U.S. Council for International Business, "protect the innovations which are the result of our extensive research, development and marketing efforts and of American artistic and intellectual creativity."[1] Innovation is crucial for economic growth and prosperity, the argument continues. Therefore, we must strengthen the property rights that protect and ultimately encourage innovation.

This statement provides a serviceable explanation of the rationale underlying most intellectual property laws. It fails, however, to clarify important theoretical and practical differences among the various kinds of intellectual properties—differences that must be understood to evaluate the importance of individual intellectual property rights and the significance of their violation.

The economics of intellectual property rights is characterized by a great many unanswered and neglected questions. Interest in intellectual property rights among economists has been sporadic and interrupted by large periods of virtual neglect. The last flurry of interest occurred in the late 1950s. One consequence is a marked absence of well-established, empirically tested relationships to support or refute many theoretical propositions. Few economists have even attempted to speculate on the theoretical framework and issues associated with international protection. Thus the economics of intellectual property rights, though not a new question, is still in its infancy.

Patents

Government grants of exclusive property rights to inventors date back to the fourteenth century, but their purpose has varied throughout history. Law in fifteenth-century Venice as well as in sixteenth-century England and the German princely states awarded inventors of "new arts" and machines and took both utility and novelty into account. Somewhat ironically, some evidence suggests that these early monopoly grants were also designed to liberate innovators from the stifling constraints imposed by the guilds. Early law in the American colonies served primarily to encourage foreign manufacturers to establish new industries in the colonies by guaranteeing them protected local markets.

By the late 1500s the English monarchy increasingly used monopoly privileges to reward court favorites, to secure loyalty, to raise money, and to control industry—not to encourage invention. Opposition to these practices precipitated the creation by the English Parliament in 1623 of the Statute of Monopolies, generally considered the model for most modern patent law. The statute outlawed the awarding of monopoly privileges except for the "first and true inventor" of a new manufacture.

From the mid-seventeenth through the mid-nineteenth century, similar laws spread throughout Europe and North America. Patent privileges were not established without opposition, however. A strong antipatent movement, particularly from 1850 to the 1870s, kept debate on the patent principle alive and, in fact, achieved the repeal of patent laws in Holland. Antipatent forces complained of the devastating effects of monopolistic privileges on world trade and emphasized the disadvantages to smaller and less advanced countries. Economic depression in the 1870s, the rise of nationalism and protectionism, and the willingness of patent advocates to compromise brought on a collapse of the antipatent forces in the last decades of the nineteenth century.

In separate studies on patents, Fritz Machlup and Edith Penrose identify four major arguments used by early supporters of a patent system.[2] The first, the "natural rights" argument, extended moral and philosophical arguments for individual property rights to intellectual properties. The position was particularly popular in nineteenth-century France. The second argument, labeled the "reward by monopoly" thesis by Machlup, carried considerable weight among early English economists. It too invoked natural rights and moral imperatives, maintaining that society owed inventors their just rewards for services rendered to society. The third, the "monopoly profits incentives" thesis, stressed that monopoly privileges or patent rights, whether just or not, were necessary economic incentives to encourage inventive activity and its financial support. Finally, others emphasized that regardless of social incentives to invent, monopolistic property rights were necessary to encourage inventors to "disclose their secrets" to society, to make their discoveries public. Patents were therefore essential for the diffusion of technology.

Modern arguments for the patent system almost completely ignore the first two positions, although new technologies are stimulating a revival of some of those issues. Early debate about whether there should be a property in a technological idea has almost completely vanished—lawyers consider the question solved. The question has recently reappeared, however, in the context of north-south debates and in controversies surrounding new technologies.

Few today would argue that patents guarantee a just reward to the inventor. The financial gains obtained through a patent bear little relation to the effort and costs expended in the invention's creation or to its usefulness to society. Moreover, inventions grow out of a social stream of intellectual developments. Patents ascribe degrees of merit to individual participants in that process in an arbitrary and, some would argue, clearly unjust manner.

Most modern arguments for the patent system rely on the final two justifications. First, patents guarantee profits and thereby secure incentives for inventors. Economists start with the recognition that knowledge goods—inventions—have awkward properties that differentiate them from the standard goods in neoclassical economic theory. Inventions often generate significant external or spillover effects. The total benefits to society of any one invention may greatly exceed the benefits indicated by the monetary compensation won by the inventor. Indeed, the price mechanism of the market completely fails to operate efficiently in the case of inventions.

The problem stems from the public character of inventions as well as the cost structure underlying their production and distribution. Inventions are public goods, characterized by difficulty of exclusion or the so-called free-rider problem—it is difficult to prevent people from consuming the goods without paying for them. Further, although the initial production costs may be significant, the distribution cost of knowledge—the idea or invention—is zero or near zero. The distribution of an additional unit of knowledge goods does not diminish the stock of those goods. The marginal cost of the additional unit will therefore be influenced not by production costs but only by distribution costs, which are insignificant. According to static economic criteria, the optimum market price for the knowledge or invention, once produced, should be roughly zero. The normal functioning of the market thus poses a problem of appropriability for the inventor. At a normal selling price of near zero, there is no incentive to produce knowledge goods.

Intellectual property rights or patents grant the inventor a temporary monopoly over the use of his or her invention and prevent competitors from sharing the knowledge without payment. They thus compensate for market failure and thereby solve the problem of appropriability. Monopoly profits or, more accurately, quasi-rents enable inventors to secure their economic interests, to cover costs, and to make a profit. (A rent is the payment that accrues to a fixed factor input. A quasi-rent is the payment that accrues to a temporarily fixed factor input—in this case the invention.) Patents thus restore economic incentives for the production of inventions. Static economic efficiency or optimal resource allocation is violated in the short term in an effort to generate a continuing supply of inventions. Dynamic economic efficiency, or efficiency associated with technological innovation, is consequently facilitated.

Because of appropriability problems, pressures to keep new discoveries secret are strong. Patent guarantees also encourage inventors to make their discoveries known and available to society and thereby promote the diffusion of technology.

The consensus among economists is that inventions do pose problems of market failure, externalities, and appropriability. Economists are somewhat less united, however, in their support for the proposed solution to the problems: the patent system. A number of factors contribute to their hesitation to endorse patents wholeheartedly. Many theoretical and practical problems associated with any patent system will never be conclusively resolved by economists. These include "what if" questions requiring observations from nonexistent patent-free environments, such as, How does innovative activity fare in a patent-free environment? Other questions are qualitative and, again, not conducive to objective, conclusive analyses. For example, do patents encourage the production of certain kinds of innovations to the detriment of others?

The patent question is ultimately one of social welfare. The patent system imposes certain costs and provides certain benefits to society. Ideally, the system would be designed to maximize net benefits to society. Most outstanding questions concern the relative magnitudes of the social costs and benefits associated with any patent system. Although economists are quick to point out the system's flaws, most agree that patents are the best of a very limited range of possible solutions. Jewkes, Sawers, and Stillerman's observation is instructive: "It is almost impossible to conceive of any existing social institution so faulty in so many ways. It survives only because there seems to be nothing better."[3]

Among the questions raised about patents is whether they actually generate the benefits attributed to them in theory—whether they increase net inventive activity. The pure impulse to invent cannot be correlated simply with anticipated monetary rewards.[4] The question of what stimulates invention remains unsettled. Others counter that invention in the classic sense of the isolated individual inventor is largely irrelevant in today's economic and corporate system. What truly matters is innovation, including investment, large-scale research and development, marketing, and commercialization, all of which certainly depend heavily on expected returns.

Patents, it has been argued, may often be unnecessary to guarantee sufficient returns to stimulate innovation. Competition itself may be sufficient incentive. Stewart and others note that knowledge transfer is in reality not instantaneous or costless.[5] The successful use of technological innovations often requires a degree of know-how that must be mastered over time. A learning curve does, in fact, exist. Innovators can gain a lead time over competitors that may usually be adequate to cancel the appropriability problem. Moreover, competition may in itself be enough to encourage disclosure in most important instances. If it is, patents bring no new benefits to society, only additional costs. Further, even if patents clearly encourage the development of new technological knowledge, it is not clear that this knowledge generates any more social benefits than knowledge that is not patentable—which the system de facto discourages.

On the cost side, patents generate the usual static inefficiencies associated with monopolies, such as higher prices, restricted supplies, and inefficient allocation of resources. Some have questioned whether there is a further negative synergism between monopoly rights and market structure, generating greater and greater market concentration and inefficiency.[6] Concern has also been raised over the market power patents may bestow on a firm in nonpatent markets. Patents cause others to invent around new technologies and thus waste scarce resources (although some have argued that this process stimulates creativity and inventiveness). Finally, the administrative costs are not insignificant.

A fundamental contradiction is inherent in any patent system, reflecting its goal of balancing conflicting static and dynamic economic objectives or the goals of optimal resource allocation and technological change. Patents explicitly prevent the diffusion of new technology to guarantee the existence of technology to diffuse in the future. This conflict leads to many anomalies. According to Joan Robinson, any patent system is bound "to produce negative results in particular instances, impeding progress unnecessarily even if its general effect is favorable on balance."[7]

Economists remain undecided about whether patents adequately solve the problem of knowledge goods but generally support them because of past technological achievements under a patent system.

According to Penrose, "It seems that the argument that patents are necessary to induce invention and to encourage the exploitation of invention is difficult to evaluate and impossible to test adequately."[8] Although no one can establish a foolproof argument for the patent system, it is obvious that rapid technological change does occur under the system. No parallels can be drawn with real-life nonpatent systems, and no theoretical arguments are sufficiently compelling to risk establishing such a system. Arguments do exist, however, for some reform of the patent system to give it greater flexibility.

Many reform proposals focus on the length of the patent term. If monopoly rights are granted for too long or too short a period, the system will not produce substantial benefits to society. Indeed, it may produce net social losses. Ideally patent terms and thus the size of monopoly rents would be established case by case after all estimates of costs and benefits had been tallied. Most such figures, however, remain highly speculative and ultimately subjective, if at all possible to derive. Administrative costs would also make such an individually tailored system prohibitive. Patent terms are now based on a long tradition (initially equal to roughly the training life of two apprentices, fourteen years) with little economic relevance. A system of alternative patent classes has been proposed as one means of securing more rational patent terms and thereby a clearer net social advantage from the patent system.

Support for alternative means of solving the problem of knowledge goods certainly exists. Some recommend that the government directly subsidize all or certain kinds of inventive activity. Others have advocated a government-sponsored system of awards for the creators of important new technologies.

Theoretical arguments about patents become considerably more complicated once we allow for the international extension of patent rights. Patents raise difficult theoretical questions about the effect of the distribution of monopoly rents on firms, national economies, and the world economy, as well as the dynamic effect on the future distribution of monopoly rents. The issues include such controversial subjects as the importance of technologically strategic sectors to a national economy and the geographic distribution of positive and negative externalities. Most of these debates demand full papers on their own merits and cannot be adequately addressed here.

Most policy makers ignore these complicated issues and rely almost exclusively on the argument that monopoly profits create incentives for invention to defend and encourage international patent protection. Not all agree, of course, that this logic is relevant to the international patent system or to all nations, for that matter. Objections to this sort of reasoning, particularly by the developing countries, lie at the heart of many disputes on the intellectual property agenda.

Copyrights versus Patents

Monopoly privileges for authors of literary and artistic works postdate the first appearance of patents by roughly a century, having emerged first in the fifteenth century. The origin of rights in literary properties can clearly be tied to the development of the printing press. As a recent Office of Technology Assessment (OTA) study notes:

> By greatly increasing the speed and reducing the costs of reproduction, printing made it much easier to disseminate ideas. By increasing the general literacy, it also made more people susceptible to and eager to partake of such ideas. As a result, the market for information products and literary works grew and their economic value was greatly enhanced.[9]

Copyrights were created by governments to capitalize on the economic opportunities afforded by printing. They were also designed to give the monarch censorship powers over printed materials during a time of political and religious turmoil. In England a printing guild was formed, and censorship was permitted by printers in exchange for an exclusive monopoly on the right to print.

By the late seventeenth century concern over censorship had diminished while concern over the high cost of monopolies had risen in Parliament. Parliament in effect destroyed the special guild privileges in 1695. Prolonged debate led in 1709 to the creation of the Statute of Anne, characterized as the first modern copyright law. The statute reestablished monopoly rights but made them available to everyone—not just the guild—and shortened their duration. It also emphasized the authors' rights in the copyright. Similar laws appeared around the world in the wake of the English statute.

Arguments in support of copyright privileges have been formulated on the same diverse bases used to defend patents. The currently predominant economic rationale for copyright protection is that literary, artistic, and scientific works are knowledge goods that create problems of market failure, externalities, and appropriability. To encourage the production of creative works, society must secure the economic rights of their creators. Copyrights, like patents, establish a form of monopoly control that solves the problem of appropriability and thereby establishes economic incentives to create and make public artistic works.

21

While the economic logic underlying patents and copyrights is, in principle, the same, there are important differences between them. Those differences flow directly from traditional distinctions between the social costs and benefits associated with inventions and those associated with copyrighted goods. They reflect differences in the nature of inventions and artistic goods and the degree of monopoly control society must guarantee to ensure the production of each. They also reflect the very different benefits society gains from each. More recent technological developments, however, have blurred some of the traditional distinctions and thereby upset the principles underlying longstanding copyright and patent laws.

Technological innovation is the primary social benefit traditionally associated with patents. It plays a crucial role in stimulating and sustaining economic growth and prosperity by reducing costs, increasing productivity, and creating new products and new markets. Indeed, economic growth since the industrial revolution has been fueled chiefly by technological innovation. Today a country's competitive standing in the world economy rests increasingly on its innovative capacity and performance. Most analysts agree that society benefits greatly from technological innovation and should therefore encourage it.

One crucial component of innovation is invention. The market alone provides inadequate incentives to invent. Inventors need guarantees that their economic interests will be protected. An invention is an idea that permits the solution of a technological problem that is directly applicable to industry. Because of the very nature of inventions, the economic rights of inventors can be secured only by guarantee of exclusive control over the use of the idea. Anything short of total control would be insufficient. Competitors would simply copy the idea or invention and underprice the original inventor. Because of costs incurred during research and development, the inventor would be forced to charge a higher price than a competitor without the same initial costs. Inventive activity might actually be discouraged. By granting the inventor exclusive privileges, patents secure minimum standards to rectify the uncertainty of appropriability.

The availability of patents affects potential inventors unevenly. Inventors can also rely on trade secrets to protect their inventions. Whether this is indeed an option depends on a host of variables. The technological complexity of the invention and the consequent potential for reverse engineering are one consideration. The amount of associated know-how is another. So too is the commercial life span of the technology. The important point here, regardless of the means of protection chosen, is that the inventor must have control over the idea or invention to have adequate guarantees of an economic return on his or her investment.

Copyrights bring different benefits to society. Literary, artistic, and scientific works are also of vital importance to society. To a great extent they define a society. Few would deny that it is in everyone's interest to encourage their creation and dissemination, but their special characteristics coupled with the peculiar nature of the social benefits they provide require monopoly rights that differ from patent rights.

The economic rights of the artist or writer must be protected if artistic activity is to be promoted. Unlike the economic interests of the inventor, however, the economic interests of authors or artists have generally not been linked directly to the ideas or information embodied in their works. The invention and the novel idea are inextricable—they are one and the same. The copyrighted work and the information or ideas it contains are separable.

Copyrighted works, moreover, rarely contain information that is novel in the sense that a patentable invention is. They are simply original works, or "noncopies," belonging to one or more well-defined and explored media. The novelty of the idea is irrelevant. It is the expression of the idea that makes these intellectual products original or unique, and it is here that the creator's economic interests lie. Society need not and cannot protect the information or ideas of a copyrighted work; it can only protect their expression. That is what copyrights do.

Although monopoly prices will be charged for the use of an invention, it must still offer improvement if it is employed. Society stands to gain from copyrighted works only if the ideas and information they embody are widely disseminated. Copyrighted intellectual goods are not traditionally tied to the output of some other tangible product of benefit to society. The ideas or information they convey are their only product, and society gains nothing by restricting those ideas. Anglo-American copyright law explicitly reaffirms the fundamental social interest in the spread of ideas and information embodied in copyrighted works by providing for "fair use," which permits limited reproduction of copyrighted works without the author's permission for purposes of criticism, scholarship, teaching, and news reporting.

These distinctions between inventions and literary, artistic, and scientific works offer one useful means of arranging and ranking intellectual property issues, particularly as they relate to economic growth and competitiveness. The economic rationale for the protection of inventions and copyright goods is similar, but important traditional distinctions exist between the two and their associated forms of protection. Each category includes intellectual properties that have similar characteristics and generate similar social benefits and whose protection entails similar social costs. Further, the violation of each produces a distinct effect on the economy and on long-term economic competitiveness.

The practical and analytical usefulness of the distinction between copyrights and inventions has increasingly been undermined by revolutions in technology. New technologies are rendering traditional categories obsolete. First, many new technologies do not fit neatly into either conventional class of knowledge goods but have characteristics of both groups. Second, technological change has dramatically altered the industrial, economic, and social significance of traditional classes of intellectual properties. This has upset the balance between social costs and benefits that underlies intellectual property laws, challenging their structure and perhaps their very usefulness. More specifically, the demands of the so-called information age raise numerous questions about the value, ownership, and control of information and thus about the nature, scope, and applicability of copyright law.

A Note on Nonpatent Industrial Properties

The nonpatent industrial properties, such as trademarks and industrial designs, are economically different from inventions and copyright works. Although the argument that monopoly profits create incentives has been used to defend these intellectual properties, it is relevant only in a roundabout way.

These markings are used to establish product differentiation, an economic phenomenon that has stimulated much debate. On the positive side, they help improve distributional efficiency by providing information to the consumer. They can identify quality standards, the materials used, the craftsmanship expended, safety standards, and the like. As a result, they help encourage qualitative product differentiation and product diversity. Insofar as the firms that pursue improvements in quality are also the innovators, rents gained under the protected mark also support further innovation.

The protection of such marks, however, has drawbacks. It encourages the redirection of scarce resources away from productive uses toward lavish advertising programs of dubious social value. It undermines price and quality competition by encouraging image competition. Marks may help extend monopoly privileges beyond the patent term and increase private returns beyond what is socially optimal. Marks and associated advertising campaigns have also been

24

criticized for their Veblenesque effects, generating hedonistic tastes and desires throughout society.

The social costs and benefits of nonpatent industrial properties are less clear and far more uncertain than those of inventions and copyrights. It is far less certain whether the monopoly rights of nonpatent industrial properties and the social costs in the form of static inefficiencies that they create will, in fact, generate dynamic efficiencies down the line. There is a large literature on this subject, and economists have more definite opinions on these issues than on patents, partly because more empirical evidence is available to support both sides.

Notes

1. U.S. Council for International Business, *A New MTN: Priorities for Intellectual Property* (New York, 1985), p. 3.

2. Fritz Machlup, *An Economic Review of the Patent System*, study no. 15, U.S. Congress, Senate, Judiciary Committee, Subcommittee on Patents, Trademarks, and Copyrights (Washington, D.C., 1957); and Edith Tilton Penrose, *The Economics of the International Patent System* (Baltimore: Johns Hopkins University Press, 1951).

3. John Jewkes, David Sawers, and Richard Stillerman, *The Sources of Invention* (New York: St. Martin's Press, 1959), p. 251.

4. E. M. Rogers, *Diffusion of Innovation*, 3d ed. (New York: Free Press, 1982; 1st ed., 1962).

5. Frances Stewart, *Technology and Underdevelopment* (London: Macmillan, 1977).

6. M. I. Kamien and N. L. Schwartz, *Market Structure and Innovation* (Cambridge: Cambridge University Press, 1982); and Harold Fox, *Monopolies and Patents* (Toronto: University of Toronto Press, 1947).

7. Joan Robinson, *The Accumulation of Capital* (Homewood, Ill.: Richard D. Irwin, 1956), p. 87.

8. Penrose, *International Patent System*, p. 39.

9. Office of Technology Assessment, *Intellectual Property Rights in an Age of Electronics and Information* (Washington, D.C., 1986), p. 34.

5
Current Issues

The intellectual property issues on the public policy agenda might be organized in a number of ways. I have found it convenient to divide them into three rough groups. The first group consists of institutional issues confronting the existing regime. The second group, labeled old issues, includes problems related to the enforcement of traditional intellectual property rights or existing intellectual property laws and institutions. The third group, new issues, comprises questions stemming more clearly from problems posed by new technologies. Any division is, of course, arbitrary. Virtually all intellectual property issues have many facets, are extremely complex, and defy easy categorization.

Institutional Issues

A large number of outstanding questions concern the domestic and international regimes for the protection of intellectual property rights. The existing international regime has been criticized for the following reasons, among others:

- The number of signatories to specific agreements is far too low for the agreements to have any substantial effect. The agreements have no applicability, of course, in countries that are not members.
- The existing agreements provide for no enforcement powers or bodies and no means for the settlement of disputes.
- The existing agreements are far too limited in scope, leaving many crucial areas unprotected. More specifically, the agreements have failed to keep pace with technological development.
- The existing agreements generally rely on national treatment as the basis for international protection. Given the absence of a common set of rules and the wide variety of protection measures and terms of protection among nations, national treatment provides insufficient guarantees of international protection.

To what extent the existing international regime can be strengthened to rectify these problems remains an open question. Some observers have argued that vested interests and jurisdictional disputes alone preclude substantial, constructive change in the present regime. They suggest the creation of a new institutional structure for intellectual property protection. Most disagree, however, arguing that we should build on the experience and technical expertise of the existing regime.

That still leaves unanswered the questions of how international organizations with related interests, such as the General Agreement on Tariffs and Trade (GATT) and the Organization for Economic Cooperation and Development (OECD), should interact with the intellectual property organs. There is a movement in the United States to make the GATT the focal point for enforcement powers and means of settling disputes. Just how the GATT would interact with the World Intellectual Property Organization, the standards-setting body, is still unclear. So too is the question of standards in the GATT. Other countries, particularly in the developing world, do not support these efforts. They maintain that intellectual property issues belong with WIPO alone. These debates not only are influenced by practical and institutional considerations but are dominated by political considerations.

Debate continues over the optimal strategy for the United States to pursue in promoting its intellectual property interests. All strategies involve costs and benefits, many of them political, that must be assessed. It is not clear what the full range of strategic options includes. The practical and political consequences of individual strategies have not been extensively studied. Some have argued that the United States should use its influence on all fronts—bilateral and multilateral—simultaneously to promote intellectual property rights abroad. Others suggest that negotiating efforts should be more directed and that a multifront strategy creates possible conflicts. Bilateral efforts have been criticized both for undermining multilateral negotiations and for being impractical and inconsistent. Political realities, the argument states, prevent the consistent application of standards and rules bilaterally.

These issues just scratch the surface of the institutional debates in the area of international intellectual property rights. Other questions include the details of proposed new agreements and the economic and political constraints facing third world nations.

Old Issues

North versus South. Philosophical and practical differences between the industrialized nations and the developing world cut across many of the existing international intellectual property issues. The less-

27

developed countries (LDCs) take the position that Western technology is unjustly expensive. Intellectual property rights give innovators a monopoly on information that is used to exact unreasonably high prices for their knowledge and to impose severe and unwarranted restrictions on its use. These restrictions hinder the efforts of the LDCs to modernize and thereby perpetuate and strengthen the split between them and the developed nations. Some LDCs maintain that knowledge is the common heritage of mankind and should be made available at low cost. Others argue that third world development is in the interests of all nations and that technological information should be provided readily, at low cost, and with a minimum of restrictions on its use.

The industrialized nations, of course, strongly disagree. They argue that monopoly rights must be enforced to ensure proper compensation for the private innovator. Property rights establish necessary economic incentives for future technological innovation. Third world nations must recognize this fact if they want to encourage indigenous technological development as well as foreign technology transfer.

Many people in the developing countries argue that the LDCs lack more fundamental prerequisites for strong indigenous research and development and technological innovation than adequate intellectual property rights. Without proper funds, research facilities, and scientific and technical personnel, intellectual property rights make little difference. The crucial problem, they argue, is growth sufficient to begin narrowing the north-south gap—growth that is a prerequisite for spontaneous domestic technological innovation. The neat theory that intellectual property rights balance short-term social costs against longer-term dynamic benefits holds only, if at all, in the closed system. In the real world costs and benefits are spread disproportionately among nations. Short-term private benefits (monopoly profits) as well as longer-term social benefits (a continuous supply of new knowledge goods) accrue almost exclusively to the developed nations. LDCs simply endure the costs and enjoy precious few of the gains.

Spontaneous technological innovations of the kind encouraged by intellectual property rights, others argue, should not be the focus of an economic development strategy in any event. The most appropriate technologies for a developing nation are not those dictated by the nation's current mixture of capital, skilled labor, and the like (those technologies that are encouraged by the market or that have an existing "natural" market). The existing resource mixture in most third world nations would undoubtedly encourage the adoption or production of less-advanced, more labor-intensive technologies than those in the developed nations. This would solidify the technological gap between the north and south and with it the economic development gap.

The main focus of a technology policy should be not the promotion of indigenous, private technological innovation but the government-directed acquisition and diffusion of the most advanced technologies. LDCs need to practice infant industry strategies to rectify current trade disparities, and advanced technologies are crucial to those strategies. Intellectual property rights are probably not compatible with such policy priorities.

Furthermore, technology transfer from the north can be beneficial only if it can be purchased at cost-effective prices or if it stimulates sufficient linkage effects—indirect, or ripple, economic effects caused by the original change—to offset high initial costs. The south generally views intellectual property rights as negating the possibility of either. Many LDCs have therefore embarked on policies for acquiring technology whose core is reduced protection of intellectual property. Such policies generally have two interrelated components. The first consists of technology transfer policies designed to enhance LDC control over technology on more favorable terms. Measures constructed with this end in mind include strict limits on direct foreign investment or its outright prohibition, the promotion of favorable licensing agreements, joint ventures, and the like. The second component consists of weak domestic laws for protecting intellectual property, restrictive clauses in those laws, and ineffective (or nonexistent) enforcement. The Group of 77 efforts in the UN Conference on Trade and Development (UNCTAD) and WIPO reflect both components.

The developed nations argue that even if greater obstacles to indigenous technological development in the third world exist than the absence of effective intellectual property laws, stealing Western technologies is not thereby justified. The solution to the LDCs' technological woes is the development of a technological infrastructure including an educated work force. Pirating technologies, rather than fostering the growth of such an infrastructure, stifles it. Illegal technology transfers of this sort occur in a vacuum and lack the equally important transfer of training, know-how, and experience associated with legitimate transfers. The important links are eliminated, and without those links the full use of available technologies and the development of new technology cannot occur.

The developing nations raise similar complaints about copyrights. The north has conceded to some cultural and developmental arguments and priorities by permitting, in effect, global fair use clauses in the Berne Convention and the Universal Copyright Convention.

29

Tensions over copyright violations, however, remain very high. Commercial pirating continues to flourish, particularly in some of the newly industrialized countries (NICs) in Asia, costing legitimate suppliers billions of dollars annually.

Some NICs have been willing (under heavy pressure from the United States) to strengthen intellectual property rights, partly because of the growing importance of high-technology and semi-high-technology industries in those countries. A similar pattern emerged in the Eastern bloc, which refused to honor intellectual property rights until acquiring advanced Western technology became an important goal. The People's Republic of China just recently began to establish its own intellectual property laws to facilitate its plans for greater foreign investment and inflows of Western technology. The pervading trend in the south, however, has been and continues to be toward weaker and more uncertain protection of intellectual property rights.

Patents and International Conventions. International industrial property conventions do not establish specific patent rights or regulations. They establish the principle of national treatment, whereby each contracting state offers the identical protection to nationals of other contracting states that it grants to its own nationals. National laws thus establish the actual rules and regulations, which vary considerably throughout the world. National treatment, of course, is virtually meaningless in a country with weak or ineffective patent laws.

Many countries have no patent laws or place unwarranted restrictions on patent eligibility. Indonesia, for example, has no patent laws; Mexico has no patent coverage for chemicals and pharmaceuticals; Brazil, Argentina, and Colombia have no patents for some industries; and Costa Rica reserves the right to nullify patents in the national interest.

Some countries, particularly in the developing world, offer inadequate patent terms. Examples include Costa Rica, one year for food, agrochemicals, and drugs; India, seven years from filing date or five years from patent grant, whichever is shorter; and Egypt, ten years for pharmaceuticals and foodstuffs.

Compulsory licensing laws that require the patentee to work the patent in the country within a short time are not uncommon and exist in developed countries like Canada and France. Failure to comply can lead to the loss of the patent or to compulsory licensing to a domestic firm, most often at below-market compensation. Numerous restrictive licensing laws also exist. Moreover, the enforcement of patent laws, again particularly in the developing countries, is often inadequate or nonexistent.

Variations in procedural requirements for obtaining patents also pose problems. The United States, for example, follows a first-to-invent rule while most other countries use a first-to-file rule. Under U.S. law an inventor can gain a patent within one year of the initial disclosure of the invention. Canada offers a grace period of two years between the first disclosure of a scientific discovery and a patent application. Japan and Australia provide for shorter grace periods and enforce restrictions on the kinds of publication eligible under rules governing grace periods.

In Europe, however, any disclosure before a patent application has been filed violates the criterion of novelty and effectively disqualifies the invention from eligibility for protection. Cohen-Boyer, in one such case, gained a patent on the rDNA technique but was denied protection in Europe and thereby suffered a considerable loss of royalties. A recent OECD report advocated international recognition of a six-month grace period between the first publication of scientific research results and a patent application. Some Europeans still object to first-to-invent rules as introducing too many ambiguities and uncertainties into the patent application process.

Other procedural requirements are used to delay the provision of patent rights to foreigners or to provide domestic inventors with clear advantages over their foreign rivals. Japan, for example, used procedural requirements to delay for ten years a patent on an optical fiber sought by the Corning Company. In the meantime a competitive product was developed by a Japanese firm. Europeans complain about U.S. rules that permit an American inventor to block a foreign patent application by claiming prior invention, even in the absence of published proof. Foreign inventors cannot use the same procedure to challenge American patent applications if their "prior inventive activity" occurred outside the United States.

Patented processes have their own unique problems. In some instances (chemicals, for example) only the production process, not the product, is eligible for patent protection. Protection of patented processes is defined in such a way that minor changes in a process legally constitute a new process. Infringement of a patented process, furthermore, is extremely difficult to prove. In the United States the patentee has the burden of proof. U.S. courts often lack the power to obtain the foreign records necessary to prove a patent violation. Infringement may therefore be impossible to establish.

Patents and U.S. Law. Aspects of U.S. domestic patent law have also been considered handicaps for U.S. firms on the international market. Although Congress addressed some of these problems during the closing months of the Ninety-eighth Congress, whether they addressed them satisfactorily has yet to be determined.

The United States lacks adequate protection, for example, against imports produced with infringed patented processes. The only remedy for a U.S. firm is section 337 of the Tariff Act. Germany, Great Britain, Japan, and France all have laws explicitly forbidding the importation of such goods. The Patent Law Amendments Act of 1984 adds to the exclusive rights of a process patent holder the right to exclude others from importing into the United States products made with that patent.

U.S. manufacture of the material components of a U.S. patented product by a non–patent holder has not constituted patent infringement when components were for assembly and sale abroad. Only when the product was assembled in the United States has a violation occurred. Foreign firms have simply assembled offshore and exported back to the United States. The Patent Law Amendments Act of 1984 begins to correct this problem.

Required regulatory reviews often cut significantly into the legal protection term of a patent, during which time the patentee is unable to use the innovation. Drug firms in particular have argued that such time lost should be restored to the patent term. The Drug Price Competition and Patent Term Restoration Act of 1984 restored half the regulatory review time, not to exceed five years, to the patent term.

Infringement proceedings in the United States have been criticized as inefficient, too expensive, and extremely unpredictable. Patent infringement is often difficult to prove. Injunctions are rarely granted. In the meantime the alleged violator continues to sell its products. Damages eventually awarded rarely compensate for losses.

The United States lacks a "petty," or "utility model," patent. Such patents are used for innovations that are not sufficiently novel for standard patent protection, are not worth the time and expense required to obtain a standard patent, or have a short commercial life that renders standard patents useless. Japan and Germany have such options. The Patent Law Amendments Act of 1984 establishes a system of "statutory invention registration" (SIR), or defensive patents. The SIR gives the inventor the same rights provided by patents to prevent others from patenting the invention. It does not, however, stop others from using or selling the invention. The SIR may serve as a basis for a priority claim in foreign patent applications under the Paris Convention. Authors of the new law maintain that the SIR will cost less and take less time to obtain than traditional patents.

Under current law patent licensees can negotiate an agreement, then use the license commercially and simultaneously challenge the validity of the patent. This procedure permits them to withhold agreed upon royalties.

The Freedom of Information Act has been used to obtain trade secret information now in the U.S. government's hands. Safeguards against misuse of the act are inadequate and need to be strengthened.

Antitrust per se laws have been applied in patent licensing cases, imposing unwarranted restrictions on licensing agreements. Under the per se approach courts automatically assume that certain licensing arrangements violate antitrust law without extensive inquiry into the precise effects of the particular action or whether there were valid business reasons for it.

Copyrights. Some of the most important copyright issues have arisen because of new technologies. Old-fashioned copyright infringement (now made markedly simpler by new technologies) continues to be a monumental problem. A survey by CBS in 1984 of executives in the U.S. motion picture and television, prerecorded entertainment, publishing, and advertising industries found copyright infringement the most frequently mentioned barrier to trade.[1] In fact, all those surveyed listed copyright infringement as a problem.

The U.S. Department of Commerce estimates the value of the pirated share of the world market for prerecorded music at $1.2 billion annually. The International Intellectual Property Alliance estimates U.S. losses in the recorded music industry as a consequence of piracy at $600 million.[2] Estimates of losses to U.S. book publishers due to piracy reach $700 million a year.

Asia, North Africa, and the Middle East are the principal piracy offenders, with Asia leading the pack. The International Federation of the Phonographic Industry (IFPI), for example, estimates that Singapore accounts for 40 percent of world exports of illegal music tapes.[3] South Korea, Thailand, Hong Kong, Malaysia, Indonesia, the Philippines, and others have been identified by the United States as leading violators. U.S. copyright industries lose more than $1.3 billion annually from the piracy of the top ten violators alone.[4]

Copyright problems mirror industrial property problems. Laws are national and are enforced accordingly. In some countries laws do not exist, are weak, or are not enforced.

The United States faces the additional problem of not belonging to the primary international copyright convention, the Berne Convention. This undermines American credibility as a serious champion of world copyright protection.

Trademark Counterfeiting. Counterfeiting is defined by the U.S. International Trade Commission (ITC) as the unauthorized use of a registered trademark on a product that is identical or similar to the product for which the trademark is registered and used. A recent ITC study found the following:[5]

- Counterfeiting has spread from traditionally counterfeited, highly visible, strong-brand-name consumer goods to a wide variety of consumer and industrial goods.
- The incidence of counterfeiting in each affected industry sector increased during the 1980–1982 period.
- Significantly affected industry sectors include wearing apparel and footwear, chemicals and related products, transportation equipment and accessories, miscellaneous metal products, machinery and electrical products, records and tapes, sporting goods, and miscellaneous manufactures such as luggage, jewelry, electronic games, and sunglasses. Evidence of counterfeiting of food and beverages and tobacco products was also found.
- Sales lost to foreign product counterfeiting increased from $37.5 million to $49.2 million from 1980 to 1982 (these are estimated minimum losses). Export markets affected span the globe, with the Far East most affected.
- Related violations include unregistered trademarks, copyright infringement, patent infringement, unauthorized use of a trademark on a substantially nonsimilar product, "passing off," or use of a similar but not identical trademark on a substantially similar product, and "gray market" or parallel sales of products bearing an authorized trademark in contravention of a marketing agreement.
- Minimum estimated total domestic and export sales lost because of counterfeiting and related violations were $6 billion to $8 billion in 1982. Other estimates by the International Anti-Counterfeiting Coalition and the U.S. Customs Service place U.S. losses near $20 billion.
- Approximately 131,000 jobs were lost because of counterfeiting and related violations in the five industry sectors most subject to these violations in 1982.
- The United States is the largest market for foreign counterfeiting of U.S. products.

No single international agreement explicitly deals with counterfeiting, although a number of intellectual property agreements address the problem in some manner. In the United States the Lanham Act is the chief anticounterfeiting measure. The recently passed Trademark Counterfeiting Act of 1984 strengthened the Lanham Act by making it a federal crime to traffic in counterfeit goods. Additional U.S. provisions can be found in the Food, Drug, and Cosmetic Act, the Piracy and Counterfeiting Act (covering records and tapes), and the Mail and Wire Fraud statutes.

Most foreign countries have anticounterfeiting laws, and many also have laws prohibiting the importation of counterfeit goods. The strength of those laws varies greatly, however. More to the point, evidence gathered by the ITC suggests that enforcement of anticounterfeiting laws is minimal or nonexistent, especially in the developing nations.

Progress has been made on a GATT anticounterfeiting code. The issue will be taken up in the new GATT round beginning in September 1986.

New Issues

The Growing Importance of Information. A recent report by the U.S. Office of Technology Assessment stated that

> although Congress has always had to reckon with technological change, the new information and communications technologies available today are challenging the intellectual property system in ways that may only be resolvable with substantial changes in the system or with new mechanisms to allocate both rights and rewards. Once a relatively slow and ponderous process, technological change is now outpacing the legal structure that governs the system.[6]

Indeed, the rate of innovation in communications and information technologies has outpaced that in almost every other field in any other period in history. The effect of these developments has been profound.

Communications and information technologies have changed the economic and social significance of information in ways that are just beginning to be understood. For example, communications and information services are crucial to the high-technology goods and services industries—industries that contribute significantly to growth of output, advances in productivity, low growth of prices, and the trade performance of an economy. These technologies have played a crucial role in the growth and worldwide expansion of services trade.

Improvements in the telecommunications infrastructure have sparked a dynamic process of economic and social change. They profoundly affect the allocation of capital and other resources both domestically and internationally, altering the relative values of individual resources. The shifting resource values influence the speed and di-

35

rection of future changes in technology. The new telecommunications systems have eroded national borders and have reduced individual governments' ability to forge independent macroeconomic policies. The communications revolution, in short, is altering the very foundations of modern society and the economic, social, and strategic importance of information.

Nations today have an increasing stake in the generation of a wide variety of information goods and control over them. Age-old solutions to the questions of ownership, protection, and control must be reevaluated. The rise in the value of information has upset the balance between social costs and benefits underlying many traditional intellectual property laws—a balance that will not easily be restored.

The heightened value of all sorts of information has raised some fundamental questions about intellectual property laws, particularly copyright laws. U.S. domestic copyright law and international copyright agreements have generally denied protection for information or ideas and have concentrated on the expression of ideas. Medium-by-medium protection rules therefore dominate the copyright legal terrain. This approach has become increasingly ineffective as communications media have evolved into complicated interconnected networks. Many forms of copyright protection are now partial and often uncertain.

Do existing copyright principles sufficiently reflect the social costs and benefits of information today—are they appropriate for the competitive environment of the information age? Are there legitimate property interests in nonpatent information? what kinds of nonpatent information? Can copyright law be changed to protect such information, or must wholly new forms of protection be created for that purpose? How can the ownership of nonpatent information be determined? What are the economic rights of information owners? What forms of protection would be sufficient to ensure the production of such information? If new forms of information or knowledge are protected, how should they be priced? Should monopoly rights be awarded, or should the state ensure compulsory licensing at, say, preset royalty fees? If preset fees are adopted, how will they be set, and who will set them, distribute them, and, most important, pay them?

Communications technologies, particularly the computer, have complicated copyright protection for data bases. Data bases such as dictionaries and encyclopedias have been eligible for copyright protection in the United States and many other countries. Data bases stored in computers presumably warrant equal protection. But copyright law protects the format of the information, not the information per se. Minor variations or manipulations of data sets may be sufficient to negate copyright protection. The computer makes such manipulations infinitely easier. Should the protection of computerized data bases focus, in some way, on the data instead of the signal?

These questions may be academic given the enormous problem of enforcement the computer raises. It is virtually impossible to monitor computer networks and computer activity. This problem promises to increase in complexity with the advent of even newer technologies, integrated services digital networks (ISDNs), and the expanded use of data communications networks. Finally, how does "fair use" apply to electronic data bases?

The issue of data ownership and control overlaps issues of national sovereignty and international trade, particularly for services. Nation-states have always defended their sovereign right to govern the information both entering and leaving their borders, not only for economic but for social, cultural, and political purposes. It is increasingly difficult for governments to control the flow of information across their borders, although many are enacting legislation to attempt to do so.

Unregulated information flows conflict directly with the political philosophy of many Marxist-Leninist states, which view information control as a prerequisite for creating "the socialist man and society," and thus raise additional East-West tensions. Developing nations object to the "cultural imperialism" of the industrialized north and the negative "demonstration effects" that such one-sided information flows are said to foster. Western industrial nations also risk and fear losing control over their own communications networks. The protection of individual privacy and data and military and economic security, for example, are directly tied to information ownership and regulation.

Despite almost universal concurrence on the sovereign right of a nation to control the flow of information across its borders, no consensus exists on what kinds of information are included. Further, the question whether the communications revolution has made or is making such control technically impossible must now be addressed.

Commercial considerations heighten the issue. Many international services industries, including banking, insurance, construction, and advertising, rely heavily on data flows and manipulation. Government rules covering data flows for whatever reason form nontariff barriers to trade, costing these industries billions of dollars.

The question of information ownership takes on peculiar dimensions when viewed from the perspective of the nation-state. For the most part, only the developed nations have the ability to collect, order, store, and distribute information. Other nations must then obtain access. Do those nations need to pay for that information? what kinds of information? what about information about a country's own resources? Do the sheer technical capabilities of a country give it the right to gather information about another country without its consent? Should users of satellites for data collection, for example, pay a fee? Who really owns that information? Do developmental considerations argue for special treatment for developing nations?

Satellites raise another host of intellectual property issues. One issue concerns the question of so-called private use and satellite transmission. In the landmark *Betamax* decision, the Supreme Court ruled that the public is not required to pay for video reception and recording for private use. The Satellite Television Industry Association argues that the unauthorized reception of unsupported satellite signals is a similar phenomenon and should therefore also be free. Others, of course, disagree and have attempted to circumvent the problem directly by scrambling their broadcasts.

Recent developments in satellite technology threaten to unravel the fabric of the existing international telecommunications regime. Direct broadcasting satellite (DBS) technology may soon permit high-powered satellite transmissions direct to individual homes. Such signals might be transnational and unfiltered and might thereby destroy nations' ability to regulate them.

DBS technology has raised additional issues. The Brussels Convention extended copyright protection to satellite broadcasts but did not include DBS. Can and should protection be extended here? Reception technology has made great strides in the past few years, and midpowered satellites may have capabilities previously limited to DBS. The existing regulatory framework distinguishes between the two, but technology may soon render the distinction obsolete.

The application of copyright law to satellites is generally unclear. Satellite transmission involves two steps: an up leg (ground to satellite) and a down leg (satellite to ground). International conventions view the down leg as the act of broadcasting and thus the relevant focus of protection. The up leg, some argue, is not intended for reception and is therefore not eligible for copyright protection. But what is the situation if the up-leg and down-leg parties are not the same?

Technological advances have also nullified existing international agreements for dividing orbit slots in outer space for DBS and for establishing frequencies and signal strengths. At the 1977 and 1979 World Administrative Radio Conferences countries agreed to a plan that gave each a cone of transmission designed to minimize overlap, but spillover occurred soon after and continues to expand. This and other issues in the satellite area remain outstanding. Access to limited slots in the Geostationary Arc and their regulation and the future regulatory role of the International Telecommunications Satellite Consortium (Intelsat) in global satellite communications are just two issues of great importance that are relevant to the protection of intellectual properties.

Video recording technologies have stimulated a great deal of controversy. The main question is whether reproduction of videographic works for personal use, free of charge, should be permitted. The solution to this problem in the Anglo-American copyright tradition necessarily involves the balancing of intellectual property owners' rights against the public's right to information. The U.S. Supreme Court ruled in the *Betamax* case that the public does indeed have the right to make video recordings for personal use, free of charge. Once copying is permitted for personal use, however, copying for commercial purposes may be impossible to stop. Piracy problems similar to those faced by the record and tape industries arise. Some have suggested that the creators of videograms and sound recordings be protected by a single standard compensatory royalty (German law employs such a standard); fees would be established on the basis of the recording equipment involved. The question arises of who should set, collect, and receive such royalties and what their relevance would be internationally.

The Protection of New Technologies. A few of the most important new technologies do not fit clearly into any of the existing categories of intellectual property. Their eligibility for legal protection is consequently uncertain. It is questionable whether any of the traditional intellectual property right laws would in fact be adequate or appropriate. These technologies may force a reevaluation and redefinition of existing intellectual property right classifications and forms of protection.

Computer software. Since 1969 the software and allied product markets have been the fastest growing computer markets. Because software, though expensive to develop, is relatively easy to copy, the industry is wide open to attack by pirate companies. A recent study by Future Computing, in cooperation with the Association of Data Processing Service Organizations and eleven publishers of software, estimated that piracy cost the U.S. software industry $1.3 billion in lost revenues between 1981 and 1984 and might cost $0.8 billion more in 1985.[7] In one instance Synapse Software reported that copies of its software reached Europe by phone lines before its own shipments arrived. In another instance, when market analysts for MicroPro International Corporation examined the Brazilian market, they found copies of their software already for sale.

Computer software does not fit neatly into traditional intellectual property categories. A trend has been emerging in a number of countries, including the United States, Germany, and the United Kingdom, to protect software through copyright law.[8] Other countries, however, are not convinced that copyrights are an appropriate means of protection. Australian courts originally rejected the applicability of copyright law to software; the legislature changed the law to include software in 1984. Strong forces in Japan led by the Ministry of International Trade and Industry (MITI) also argued against copyright extension. The relevance of copyright principles and protection measures for computer software is still vigorously debated in many countries.

Those favoring copyright protection argue that computer software is created like other copyright works, by placing symbols in a medium. Software is simply another form of writing brought about by technical change, as were sound recordings and motion pictures, and copyright should be extended as it was in those cases.

Others argue that only the source code, written in eye-legible form, is protectable. Software in its mature phase—the object code—is addressed to machines, not human beings; it therefore differs from writings and is not copyrightable. Some accept this distinction but support copyright for the object code provided that the program is published and that copies in a form readable by human beings are registered.

The copyrightability of the object code has also been supported on the basis that it is analogous to a "set of instructions for mechanical work," which is copyrightable. Others disagree on the grounds that printed instructions explain how to do something but programs are able to do it. The instructions of the software become part of the machine itself.

MITI, the Brazilian government, and many others have rejected the notion that copyrights are the appropriate means of protecting computer software. Since the mental and financial effort supporting the production of software resembles inventive activity more than artistic creation, industrial property laws may be more relevant than copyrights. Furthermore, software is more like industrial property than artistic works in the way it functions. To extend copyrights would be an arbitrary act that would completely ignore the special needs of software producers and society—needs that are the direct result of the industrial property qualities exhibited by software.

Most readily admit, however, that patent law also does not fit software. The core technology and methods for creating software—that is, the patentable components—are well established. It would be virtually impossible to prove the novelty or nonobviousness of software. Most opponents of copyright protection for software therefore argue for sui generis law. What are needed are measures that reflect software's functional qualities and peculiar technical characteristics. The law must take into consideration the high costs as well as the invention-like characteristics of creating software. It must also reflect the specific economic-industrial purpose of software, which distinguishes it from traditional copyright goods. With these considerations in mind, Japan initially proposed a computer software measure that embodied attributes of both patent and copyright law. Brazil, the Soviet Union, and Greece are considering similar measures.

Official U.S. opposition to protection measures other than copyright for software is based on two chief objections. First, such proposals usually provide for shorter periods of protection than offered by copyright law. Although copyrights generally offer protection for at least fifty years, the Japanese measure, for example, provided for fifteen years and the Brazilian for only ten years. Second, such measures establish software as an industrial property, placing it under the Paris Convention and making it subject to compulsory licensing.

U.S. pressures helped produce the withdrawal of the Japanese software proposal. Congressional threats to pass legislation permitting the United States to treat software producers from particular foreign countries in accord with the treatment given to American software producers in those countries has also prompted some governments to consider software copyright proposals. Singapore and Taiwan, for example, both eager to develop domestic software industries and both centers of software piracy, are now considering such laws.

Even universal acceptance of copyright protection, however, would leave important questions unanswered. Copyrights protect forms of expression, not ideas themselves or so-called methods of expression. In the U.S. court cases the software packages under contention were taken over, part and parcel, from the original. Often, however, packages can be altered slightly (for example, by changing the order of commands) while the substance of the original software is preserved. Hundreds of nonidentical programs for a video game, for example, may produce the same on-screen result. Do copyrights just protect the order of codes of the software? If so, they may not be of much economic value to the software creator, who is more interested in protecting his or her idea or final product.

Systems software that enables the computer to carry out internal organizational tasks among various parts of the computer raises additional questions. The sole audience of this software is the hardware. Some maintain that this fact alone violates the literary works criterion for copyrights and makes such software ineligible for protection. Systems software establishes only methods of operation, which are not copyrightable. Since the core technology and methods are well established, a claim of nonobviousness or novelty for software that guides the inner workings of the computer cannot be maintained. Identifying systems software is also difficult since codes (electric pulses and so on) are unintelligible to human beings. The special difficulties associated with systems software are being further compounded with the advent of "firmware"—semiconductor chips that have both applications and systems software encoded on them.

Semiconductor chips. The problems created by the piracy of semiconductor chips resemble, in some ways, the software problem. The cost of designing and preparing masks for chip manufacture can reach $100 million. Photocopying each layer of the chip and reproducing it, however, are fairly simple and can be done for less than $50,000.[9] Firms will not and cannot continue to invest large sums in chip design unless adequate safeguards against piracy are established.

Traditional intellectual property laws do not appear appropriate or adequate for the semiconductor chip. Since the basic technology for constructing chips is well established, it is argued, patents are inappropriate for chip protection. A patent could protect the technology of a new microprocessor but could not protect the layouts and artwork necessary to adapt the technology to industrial uses. It is the design work that is expensive and most susceptible to piracy. Some still have continued to argue that the design effort and the research and development involved in chip protection more resemble the effort underlying inventions and, novelty and nonobviousness tests notwithstanding, should be protected as such.

The applicability of copyrights to semiconductor chips has been defended and rejected on grounds similar to those used in the computer software debate. Copyrights, some have argued, should be extended to cover mask works since mask works are simply a form of technical drawings, which are copyrightable. The U.S. Congress, however, rejected this analogy and other arguments for copyright extension to semiconductor chips.

Copyrights have been used in the United States to protect schematic drawings of chip layouts. Copyright protection, however, does not prohibit others from manufacturing and selling the chip depicted in the protected drawings. Only the drawing aspects and information content are protected, not the useful article they portray. Copyright protection of this sort does not secure the economic interests of the chip creator.

Because the mask work is made for and used solely as a part of a manufacturing process—to produce a useful article, the semiconductor chip—it falls outside the traditional domain of copyrights. Copyrights can protect artistic aspects of a useful article but only when they can be separated from its utilitarian qualities. The mask work has "no intrinsic aesthetic purpose" beyond its role in chip production. Extending copyright protection to utilitarian objects would undermine the integrity and consistency of traditional copyright law. Semiconductor chips, states a congressional report, are really "a form of industrial intellectual property."[10]

For these reasons Congress decided that neither patents nor copyrights were appropriate and that a sui generis approach for semiconductor chips should be adopted. The Semiconductor Chip Protection Act of 1984 establishes intellectual property rights based on principles similar to copyright for creators of mask works. Creators are given exclusive rights over the reproduction, importation, distribution, and sale of the mask work for a period of ten years. To be eligible, the mask work must only be original, not nonobvious or novel in the patent sense, and must be registered within two years of its creation. Enforcement provisions parallel those for copyrights, establishing civil penalties. Fines may reach a maximum of $250,000, however, much higher than penalties for copyright violation. The law also permits reverse engineering for teaching, evaluation, and demonstration purposes, so as to encourage the production of competitive improvements and alternatives to individual chips. Legitimate reverse engineering and piracy are to be distinguished on the basis of the so-called paper trail associated with the process.

Whether this solution will be adequate is impossible to determine. Already speculation about new technologies promises to add further complications. Some, for example, see the eventual replacement of silicon chips by organic materials—molecular electronics. That would introduce a whole new set of intellectual property controversies. The protection of semiconductor chips remains under discussion in a number of nations.

Biotechnology. Advances in biotechnology are generally protected either by patents or trade secrets or by so-called plant breeder laws (in the United States, the Plant Patent Act and the Plant Variety Protection Act). The international system for the protection of plant breeders' rights was established in 1961 at the International Convention for the Protection of New Varieties of Plants, which is administered through WIPO. Several problems in the protection of biotechnology intellectual property rights remain.

First is the problem of national differences in patentable subject matter and patents versus plant breeder laws. U.S. patent law (as a result of *Diamond* v. *Chakrabarty*) allows for the patenting of a broad range of subject matter, including plants and animals.[11] Only tuber-propagated plants or plants found in an uncultivated state—chiefly Irish potatoes and the Jerusalem artichoke—are not patentable.

In Europe and Japan plants and animals are generally not eligible for patent protection. The European Patent Convention prohibits patent protection for "plant or animal varieties or essentially biological processes for the production of plants and animals." It does, however, allow for the patenting of "microbiological processes or the products thereof." Japanese law makes a similar distinction. The distinction is an ambiguous one that raises many questions about lower organisms and their legal status.

Uncertainties caused by European and Japanese law create many problems for U.S. inventors when they must choose between trade secrets and patents to protect their creations. Europe and Japan publish patent applications roughly eighteen months after the initial filing and before granting the patent. Such disclosure effectively negates the potential for protection under trade secret law before patent eligibility is determined. Uncertain patent eligibility in Europe and Japan also deters U.S. firms from filing for U.S. patents. Culture samples, required to obtain a U.S. patent, may be copied by foreign firms for production and sale in unprotected markets. Deposited cultures are also made available to the public in all OECD countries but the United States and Switzerland. This practice further increases the risks if patents are denied.

Recent developments in genetic research have heightened conflict over European treatment of property rights in biotechnology. Lawyers of numerous European chemical companies have argued that genetic engineering techniques are "microbiological," not "essentially biological," and can therefore be patented. Plant breeders, the Union for Protection of New Plant Varieties, and others strongly disagree. They feel that such process patents, if granted, would conflict directly with their rights as stipulated in existing plant breeder law.

Most of the controversy concerns the scope of proposed market rights for these process patents. Those advocating the extension of patents to genetic engineering techniques maintain that process protection must also cover subsequent varieties based on the new plant produced by the process. This demand directly contradicts the convention and, according to plant breeders, would pave the way for chemical companies to take over their business.

Both sides pleaded their cases during the preparation of a recent OECD report, neither side scoring a decisive victory.[12] The OECD report urges stronger protection for biotechnology but takes no stand in favor of one system or another.

Another problem is the diversity of novelty requirements. The United States follows a first-to-invent rule that provides for a one-year grace period between publication of an invention and application for a patent. European nations follow a first-to-apply rule and consider prior publication evidence sufficient to revoke novelty and thus to reject protection. This problem is particularly acute in biotechnology, where academic scientists are eager to publish results of their studies for criticism. At the urging of the OECD, some countries are considering instituting a grace period between publication and patent application.

Most European law requires a demonstration of reproduction to obtain protection for many organisms. Germany further requires a written description of a repeatable procedure for reproducing many organisms (from scratch) before granting patents. Some organisms, which have been produced by random mutation and selection that cannot be repeated with certainty, would not be eligible for protection under these laws.

New developments have created enforcement problems. Most protection covers a specific organism or part of an organism. With new technological developments, it will be or may already be possible to disguise the use of a biological invention by genetic manipulation. All these problems are compounded in the developing world, where protection for biotechnology is particularly weak.

Notes

1. CBS, *Trade Barriers to U.S. Motion Picture and Television, Prerecorded Entertainment, Publishing, and Advertising Industries* (New York, 1984), p. 1.

2. U.S. Department of Commerce, *1986 U.S. Industrial Outlook* (Washington, D.C., 1986), pp. 624–25.

3. "Pirates Repelled: Asia's Copyright Infringers Come under Attack," *Far Eastern Economic Review*, April 24, 1986, p. 58.

4. Task Force on Intellectual Property, "Recommendations of the Task Force on Intellectual Property to the Advisory Committee for Trade Negotiations" (Washington, D.C., October 1985), p. 2.

5. International Trade Commission, *The Effects of Foreign Product Counterfeiting on U.S. Industry* (Washington, D.C., 1984).

6. Office of Technology Assessment, *Intellectual Property Rights in an Age of Electronics and Information* (Washington, D.C., 1986), p. 3.

7. "Business Software Piracy," *EDS Washington Report on Federal Data Systems*, vol. 3, no. 4 (April 1985), p. 3.

8. "Who Owns the Idea?" *Omni* (March 1985), p. 35. Not all Americans are willing to accept the copyright classification for computer software. The matter has produced considerable controversy at universities, which generally distinguish between copyrights and patents produced by faculty authors, claiming patents for the university and leaving copyrights to the authors. Software created by a faculty member would seem to be the property of the faculty member. University administrators are not willing to let millions of dollars go without a fight, however, and have challenged the software classification, claiming that software resembles an industrial property and therefore belongs to the university. In a recent case that may end up in the courts, the California Institute of Technology's refusal to abandon its claim to a software package produced by a young faculty member led to his resignation and to a review by the university of its intellectual property rules. Other leading universities are following suit. The final decisions will no doubt have considerable effect on the future composition of some faculties.

9. U.S. Congress, House of Representatives, *House Report 98-781*, 98th Congress, 2d session, 1984, p. 2.

10. Ibid., p. 8.

11. Office of Technology Assessment, *Commercial Biotechnology: An International Analysis* (Washington, D.C., 1984), p. 386.

12. Organization for Economic Cooperation and Development, *Biotechnology and Patent Protection: An International Review* (Paris, 1985).

6
Summary:
The Policy Research Agenda

The problem of the international protection of intellectual property rights encompasses a range of diverse and often complex issues. The continual introduction of new technologies, particularly new information technologies, promises to complicate these matters further. For many years the sheer range and complexity of the field served to deter a concerted effort by the U.S. government to defend and actively to promote intellectual property rights abroad. As often happens, commercial considerations have now forced the government to attack the problems directly.

Many fundamental questions, however, remain unresolved. Few persons outside the legal profession have devoted much time or effort to studying the broad dimensions of intellectual property matters. As a result, the field is virtually unexplored territory for research and study.

A review of the literature suggests three broad areas as priorities for research on intellectual property issues. The first of these areas, the economics of intellectual property rights, includes research and review of the economic logic underlying the three main categories of intellectual property rights: patents, copyrights, and trademarks. Some attempt to reevaluate this logic at both the theoretical and the empirical levels must be pursued. Little effort has been made to collect comprehensive data to support intellectual property rights—data that are necessary to convince our reluctant trading partners of *their* interest in greater international protection. Data should include more refined estimates of the costs of violations of intellectual property rights.

Concentration on specific problems related to the international protection of rights is particularly needed. Here even the theoretical literature is virtually nonexistent. The social welfare implications of the protection of patents, copyrights, and trademarks may change significantly once we consider the trade dimension. The distribution of the costs and benefits of the system becomes a much greater issue, for example. The heightened importance of technology in establishing comparative advantage and a strong competitive standing in the world make our understanding of international protection all the more important. The optimal structure of an international regime and the priorities of U.S. policy both depend on this greater understanding.

The second area—the institutional dimensions of the international intellectual property regime—includes a review of the existing regime and its major problems. Studies analyzing the technical as well as the political aspects of the institutional structure are warranted. For example, is the World Intellectual Property Organization (WIPO) the appropriate focus for strengthening international intellectual property protection? Can the existing conventions and agreements under WIPO serve as a basis for a new, stronger international regime, or do the magnitude and complexity of current problems argue for the creation of a whole new system?

What role can other multilateral institutions play in an improved regime? U.S. policy makers see a significant role for the General Agreement on Tariffs and Trade (GATT) in any new regime. Are there major problems in identifying the clearly trade-related intellectual property issues? What are the political and practical implications of relying more heavily on the GATT? Would the GATT assume standards-setting duties? How would the GATT interact with other institutions with intellectual property responsibilities?

Little agreement exists concerning the content and organization of new international rules for intellectual property protection. The underlying principle of the existing system—national treatment—provides at best a minimum standard for protection. Can we successfully establish common international rules to strengthen the effects of national treatment? Can we give teeth to these rules by creating GATT-like provisions for the settlement of disputes and enforcement?

What, further, are the best means for the United States to promote its policy objectives? Dominant opinion in the public policy arena appears to support a multifaceted strategy—to use bilateral and multilateral avenues simultaneously. Can policy be consistent under such a sweeping mandate? What exactly are the pros and cons of each strategy, and where do they complement and conflict with each other? Is it politically feasible for the United States to require adequate intellectual property protection as a precondition for General System of Preferences (GSP) and most-favored-nation privileges? North-south controversies promise to pose a major stumbling block to any multilateral agreement. Is this just one more argument in support of the formation of a "super-Gatt" of like-minded trading nations?

Conflicts between the developed and the developing countries play an important role in defining the realistic potentials for U.S. policy and the international system for intellectual property protection. What are the key differences between the north and the south, and how intractable are those differences? How do they shape American policy strategies and objectives in this area?

The final priority area concerns issues related to new technologies. A few of the new and most important technologies do not fit clearly into any of the existing categories of intellectual properties. Their eligibility for legal protection is consequently also uncertain. It is questionable, further, whether any of the traditional property rights would in fact be adequate or appropriate. New technologies may force a reevaluation and redefinition of existing intellectual property classifications and forms of protection.

How can the international protection of these new technologies be ensured when the U.S. courts and the Congress have not fully resolved these problems? Should the United States simply permit other countries to work out these problems and worry about the international consequences of national solutions later? Or should we promote multilateral solutions from the outset in an effort to eliminate future disputes? Controversial new technologies include some of the most important technological developments of this century—computer software, semiconductor chips, and biotechnology. These areas deserve specialized attention because of their individual importance and for the effect they may have on the protection of future technologies.

The revolution in communications technologies and the resulting growth in the value of information have raised other profound questions in the area of intellectual property rights. New communications technologies have changed the economic and social significance of information in ways that are just beginning to be understood. Nations today have an increasing stake in the generation and control of a wide variety of information goods. Communications networks and information systems provide the infrastructure and the transportation system for today's world economy. They are, as a result, of central importance to the future health and well-being of a nation.

The rise in the value of information has upset the social cost-benefit balance underlying traditional intellectual property laws. The rapidity of technological change across sectors, for example—made possible in part by advances in computer and information technologies—has undermined the usefulness of patent protection for many industrial properties. New communications technologies directly challenge basic copyright principles. Do existing copyright principles adequately reflect the social costs and benefits of information today—are they appropriate for today's competitive environment based on information control? For example, are there legitimate property interests in some nonpatent forms of information? Current copyright law offers no protection for information per se, only for its packaging. What new kinds of information deserve protection? Can copyright law be changed to accommodate new forms of protection, or must new kinds of intellectual properties and laws be created for that purpose?

These and other complicated intellectual property questions deserve thorough study and debate. Action in the public policy arena, however, will move according to its own schedule. Important decisions concerning negotiating strategies—and, indeed, negotiations themselves—have already begun to take shape. The accelerated pace of public policy decision making increases the urgency of more reliable information on the complicated questions related to the international protection of intellectual property rights.

Appendix

Industrial Property Agreements under the World Intellectual Property Organization

Paris Convention, 1883: Ninety-two states including the United States

- covers industrial property in the widest sense—inventions, trade names, trademarks, service marks, industrial designs, utility models, indicators of source, appellations of origin, and repression of unfair competition
- provides for (1) *national treatment*—each contracting state must grant the same protection to nationals of other contracting states as it grants to its own nationals; (2) *right of priority*—once an application for protection is filed in one country belonging to the agreement, the applicant has twelve months to file in any other contracting state, which then must regard the application as if it were filed on the same day as the original application; (3) *common rules*—prohibits the denial by a state of industrial design protection on the grounds that the article incorporating the design is not manufactured in that state; provides that protection must be awarded for trade names without registration requirements; prohibits false indications of source of goods or identity of trader or producer; requires "effective" protection against unfair competition; and provides that all rules for the application, registration, applicability, and duration of patents and trademarks are the province of individual states

Madrid Agreement (source of goods), 1891: Thirty-two states not including the United States

- provides for confiscation upon importation, prohibition of imports, or other appropriate measures against goods bearing false or deceptive indications of source

Madrid Agreement (registration of marks), 1891: Twenty-five states not including the United States

- provides for the registration of marks with WIPO, which then handles the filing to individual states in which registration is desired

Hague Agreement, 1925: Seventeen states not including the United States

- provides for the international deposit of industrial designs

Nice Agreement, 1957: Thirty-two states including the United States

- divides the registration of marks into thirty-four classes for goods and eight for services
- is designed to facilitate international registration of marks by establishing worldwide uniformity

Lisbon Agreement, 1958: Sixteen states not including the United States

- provides for protection of appellations of origin

International Convention for the Protection of New Varieties of Plants, 1961: Seventeen states including the United States

- creates the Union for Protection of New Plant Varieties (UPOV)
- establishes a system of international protection for breeders of new plant varieties
- provides for *national treatment, right of priority*, and *common rules*, including the following: protection must be granted in the form of special titles or patents; protection must be granted to the largest possible number of genera and species; protection covers the use of the plant variety for production for commercial use, offerings for sale, and marketing but does not cover use to create other new varieties; the variety must be clearly distinguishable from other varieties; and protection must be provided for at least fifteen years

Locarno Agreement, 1968: Fifteen states not including the United States

- establishes thirty-one classes and 211 subclasses of industrial design
- seeks to establish worldwide uniformity to facilitate international registration of industrial designs

Patent Cooperation Treaty (PCT), 1970: Thirty-two states including the United States

- provides for the filing of an international patent application, whose effect in each member state is the same as if a national patent application had been filed
- provides for international search to determine novelty
- is designed to increase efficiency and reduce the costs of international patenting

52

International Patent Classification (IPC) Agreement, 1971: Twenty-seven states including the United States

- divides technologies into eight main classifications and approximately 52,000 subdivisions, each of which is assigned a symbol
- is designed to establish worldwide uniformity of classifications to facilitate international patenting

Trademark Registration Treaty, 1973: Five states not including the United States

- is similar to IPC Agreement, but covers trademarks

Budapest Treaty, 1977: Twelve states including the United States

- covers the patenting of microorganisms
- provides that applicants need deposit a culture sample only with one authorized "international depository authority"

Nairobi Treaty, 1981: Six states not including the United States

- prohibits commercial use of the Olympic symbol without the sanction of the Olympic committee and, generally, compensation to the committee

Other International Industrial Property Agreements

European Patent Convention (EPC), 1973: Eleven states of the European Economic Community (EEC)

- creates universal standards for granting patents in eleven Western European nations and establishes a European patent
- does not, however, establish uniform national patent protection laws; the European patent is subject to the existing patent laws of the individual countries

Council for Mutual Economic Assistance (CMEA) Agreement, 1976: Ten socialist states

- provides for "title of protection" to be granted and to carry equal force in all contracting states
- provides for right of priority

Copyright Agreements under WIPO

Berne Convention, 1886: Seventy-four states not including the United States

- covers the protection of literary and artistic works
- establishes three main principles: (1) national treatment,

53

(2) nonconditional protection, and (3) protection independent of the existence of protection in the country of origin

• provides for the following minimum standards of protection: "works" include every production in literary, scientific, and artistic domains, whatever the mode of expression; rights of authorization must include (subject to permitted reservations) the rights to translate, to perform in public, to broadcast, to make reproductions, to make motion pictures, and to make adaptations and arrangements; protection must extend for fifty years beyond the death of the author, except where exceptions are permitted; less-developed countries (LDCs) may depart from minimum standards; works are subject to compulsory licensing in LDCs for purposes of teaching, scholarship, or research, but the export of copies made under such compulsory licensing arrangements is prohibited

Rome Convention, 1961: Twenty-three states not including the United States

• provides for protection of three categories of auxiliaries to literary and artistic creations: protects performers from having their performances broadcast or reproduced without their consent; protects producers of phonograms from their direct or indirect reproduction without consent and compensation; protects broadcasting organizations from the unauthorized use of their broadcasts
• makes all provisions subject to reservations
• is administered jointly by WIPO and the International Labor Organization (ILO)

Geneva Convention, 1971: Thirty-six states including the United States

• provides for the protection of producers of phonograms from unauthorized reproductions and the importation of such reproductions
• defines phonograms as aural fixations (not films or videos) whatever their form
• provides that protection must last at least twenty years

Brussels Convention, 1974: Seven states not including the United States

• provides for contracting states to take adequate measures to prevent unauthorized distribution on or from their territory of any program-carrying signal transmitted by a satellite
• is not applicable where distribution is made from a direct broadcasting satellite
• departs from simple national treatment

Madrid Multilateral Convention, 1979: not yet in force

• provides for the avoidance of double taxation of copyright royalties (often an author is subject to taxes in both the country where the work is exploited and his or her country of residence)
• calls for bilateral agreements or domestic laws to eliminate double taxation
• is administered jointly by WIPO and UNESCO

Other International Copyright Agreements

Mexico City Convention on Literary and Artistic Copyright, 1902: Sixteen Central and South American states and the United States—seven have ratified, including the United States

• provides for national treatment
• stipulates that the duration of the protection granted should not exceed the term granted in the country of origin

Buenos Aires Convention on Literary and Artistic Copyright, 1910: Twenty Central and South American states and the United States—nine have ratified, including the United States

• provides that works registered in accordance with laws of the state of origin shall be given the full faith and credit of the law in all other participating states without additional formalities

Inter-American Convention on the Rights of the Author in Literary, Scientific, and Artistic Works, 1946: Twenty-one Central and South American states and the United States—fifteen have ratified, not including the United States

• provides the author with exclusive rights over the diffusion of his or her work through television, radio, or any other method
• provides that the author may dispose of the copyright but still retain the right to oppose modifications of his or her work

Universal Copyright Convention, 1952: Seventy-five states including the United States

• provides for national treatment and common rules or minimum standards on copyrights
• permits individual country exceptions consistent with the "spirit" of the agreement
• provides for a minimum of protection equal to the life of the author plus twenty-five years for most works
• permits exceptions for LDCs
• constitutes a less stringent Berne Convention

Convention for the Protection of Producers of Phonograms against Unauthorized Duplication of Their Phonogram, 1971: Thirty-two states including the United States

- prohibits unauthorized duplication and the importation of unauthorized duplicates of phonograms
  - provides exceptions for educational materials
  - abandons national treatment

U.S. Domestic Law

Article I, section 8, clause 8, of the U.S. Constitution gives Congress the power to "promote the Progress of Science and useful Arts, by securing for limited times to Authors and Inventors the exclusive Rights to their respective Writings and Discoveries."

U.S. Copyright Act, 17 U.S.C. (P.L. 94-553, 90 Stat. 2541 (1976))

- protects individual works of authorship fixed in any tangible medium of expression, but only the form of expression, not ideas
- grants the author exclusive rights to the sale or reproduction of the work with exceptions for fair use; reproduction of single copies for library and archival use; works in connection with nonprofit, educational, governmental, and religious uses; certain cable system transmissions; passive carriers involved in secondary transmissions; and certain ephemeral recordings
  - protects for the life of the author plus fifty years
- provides explicitly through 1976 amendment for copyright eligibility for computer software

Patent Act of 1975, 35 U.S.C. (P.L. 93-596, 88 Stat. 1949 (1975))

- provides the creator with a short-term monopoly over the invention; protects the idea
- provides that the idea or invention must be novel, nonobvious, and useful to be patentable
- provides that an invention is ineligible for patent if patented or described in the United States or abroad, in public use, or on sale in this country more than one year before the patent application

Lanham Act (trademark law)

- forbids affixation or use of false designation of origin or false descriptions or representations in connection with any goods or services
- provides civil penalties for trademark infringement and counterfeiting

56

Trade Secrets—Most states have provisions protecting proprietors from piracy of trade secrets. The proprietor must usually prove that it made an effort to maintain confidentiality.

Tariff Act of 1930, section 337, permits the ITC to prohibit the importation of foreign goods when material injury to a U.S. firm results as a consequence of unfair trade practices, including patent and copyright infringement.

Trade Act of 1974, section 301, grants the president powers to impose import restrictions to remove any act, policy, or practice of a foreign country that violates a trade agreement or is unjustifiable, unreasonable, or discriminatory and injures or restricts U.S. commerce.

Bibliography

Barfield, Claude, and Robert Benko. "International Communications and Information Systems: The Impact on Trade." *Foreign Policy and Defense Review* 5, no. 4 (September 1985).

Basche, James R. *Regulating International Data Transmissions: The Impact on Managing International Business.* New York: Conference Board, 1984.

Block, Alex Ben. "This Is War!" *Forbes*, March 11, 1985.

The British Patent System: Report of the Committee to Examine the Patent System and Patent Law. Cmnd. 4407. London: H.M. Stationery Office, 1970.

Burstein, M. L., Lester G. Telser, Ben Yu, Michael Gort, Richard Wall, John P. Palmer, and Yoram Barzel. "Symposium on Knowledge-based Products: Innovations and Property Rights." *Economic Inquiry* 22, no. 4 (October 1984).

"Business Software Piracy." *EDS Washington Report on Federal Data Systems* 3, no. 4 (April 1985).

CBS. *Trade Barriers to U.S. Motion Picture and Television, Prerecorded Entertainment, Publishing, and Advertising Industries.* New York, 1984.

"Chemical Giants Push for Patents on Plants." *Science* 228, June 14, 1985.

"The Chip." *National Geographic* 162, no. 4 (October 1982).

"Copyright Law Revision: First since 1909." *1976 Congressional Quarterly Almanac.* Washington, D.C.: CQ Press, 1976.

Fox, Harold. *Monopolies and Patents.* Toronto: University of Toronto Press, 1947.

Freeman, Christopher. *The Economics of Industrial Innovation.* Cambridge, Mass.: MIT Press, 1982.

Gorlin, Jacques. "A Trade-based Approach for the International Copyright Protection for Computer Software." September 1, 1985.

Griliches, Zvi, ed. *R&D, Patents, and Productivity.* Chicago: University of Chicago Press, 1984.

Hill, Eileen. "U.S. Intellectual Property Rights: Commerce Department Program Seeks Greater Protection for U.S. Intellectual Property Rights." *Business America*, March 18, 1985.

Hoff, Paul. *Inventions in the Marketplace: Patent Licensing and the U.S. Antitrust Laws*. Washington, D.C.: American Enterprise Institute, 1986.

Intellectual Property Owners News, various issues.

International Trade Commission. *The Effects of Foreign Product Counterfeiting on U.S. Industry*. Washington, D.C., 1984.

Jan Yurow Associates. *Issues in International Telecommunications Policy: A Source Book*. Washington, D.C.: George Washington University Press, 1983.

Jewkes, John, David Sawers, and Richard Stillerman. *The Sources of Invention*. New York: St. Martin's Press, 1959.

Kamien, M. I., and N. L. Schwartz. *Market Structure and Innovation*. Cambridge: Cambridge University Press, 1982.

Macauley, Molly, and Paul Portney. "Property Rights in Orbit." *Regulation* (July/August 1984).

Machlup, Fritz. *An Economic Review of the Patent System*. Study no. 15, U.S. Congress, Senate, Judiciary Committee, Subcommittee on Patents, Trademarks, and Copyrights. Washington, D.C., 1957.

The Management of Transborder Data Flows: Proceedings of a Conference at Columbia University. New York: Columbia University, 1984.

Miller, Michael. "U.S. Software Firms Try to Curb Foreign Pirates to Protect Big American Share of World Market." *Wall Street Journal*, April 18, 1985.

Nakayama, Nabuhiro. "The Japan-U.S. Dispute over Software Protection." *Economic Eye* (March 1985).

National Commission on New Technological Copyrighted Works. *Final Report*. Washington, D.C.: Library of Congress, 1978.

National Commission on New Technological Uses of Copyright Works. *Economics of Property Rights as Applied to Computer Software and Data Bases*. Washington, D.C., June 1977.

Office of Technology Assessment. *Commercial Biotechnology: An International Analysis*. Washington, D.C., January 1984.

———. *Intellectual Property Rights in an Age of Electronics and Information*. Washington, D.C., 1986.

Organization for Economic Cooperation and Development. *Biotechnology and Patent Protection: An International Review*. Paris, 1985.

———. *Restrictive Business Practices Relating to Patents and Licenses: A Report by the Committee of Experts on Restrictive Business Practices*. Paris, 1972.

Penrose, Edith Tilton. *The Economics of the International Patent System*. Baltimore: Johns Hopkins University Press, 1951.

Pine, Art. "White House Seeks to Boost Protection for Patents, Copyrights, Trademarks." *Wall Street Journal*, April 8, 1986.

"Pirates Repelled: Asia's Copyright Infringers Come under Attack." *Far Eastern Economic Review*, April 24, 1986.

Polanyi, M. "Patent Reform." *Review of Economic Studies* (Summer 1944).

"The President Announces New Trade Policy." *Business America*, September 30, 1985.

President's Commission on Industrial Competitiveness. *Global Competition, the New Reality*. Washington, D.C., 1985.

Proceedings of the U.S. Copyright Office Symposium on the Sources of International Copyright Law. Washington, D.C., 1984.

"Push for European Patent Reform." *Science* 227, February 22, 1985.

Quester, George. "Transboundary Television." *Problems of Communism* (September/October 1984).

Rasheed, Jamal. "Books Too Expensive? Then Copy Your Own." *Far Eastern Economic Review*, November 7, 1985.

Robinson, Glen O., ed. *Communications for Tomorrow: Policy Perspectives for the 1980s*. New York: Praeger Publishers, 1978.

Robinson, Joan. *The Accumulation of Capital*. Homewood, Ill.: Richard D. Irwin, 1956.

Rogers, E. M. *Diffusion of Innovation*, 3d ed. New York: Free Press, 1982; 1st ed., 1962.

Scherer, F. M. *Industrial Market Structure and Economic Performance*. Chicago: Rand McNally, 1970.

Schmookler, Jacob. *Patents, Invention, and Economic Change: Data and Selected Essays*, edited by Zvi Griliches and Leonid Hurwicz. Cambridge, Mass.: Harvard University Press, 1972.

Schwartz, Harry. "The UN System's War on the Drug Industry." *Regulation* (July/August 1982).

Stewart, Frances. *Technology and Underdevelopment*. London: Macmillan, 1977.

Task Force on Intellectual Property. "Recommendations of the Task Force on Intellectual Property to the Advisory Committee for Trade Negotiations," October 1985 and March 1986.

Taylor, C. T., and Z. A. Silberton. *The Economic Impact of the Patent System: A Study of the British Experiment*. Cambridge: Cambridge University Press, 1973.

"That's Entertainment." *Business America*, August 5, 1985.

Thompson, Dennis. "The UNCTAD Code on Transfer of Technology." *Journal of World Trade Law* 16 (July/August 1982).

United Nations, Department of Economic and Social Affairs, UNCTAD Secretariate, and the International Bureau of WIPO. *The Role of the Patent System in the Transfer of Technology to Developing Countries*. New York, 1975.

U.S. Congress. *Conference Report 98-1156*. 98th Congress, 2d session, 1984.

U.S. Congress. House of Representatives. *House Report 98-781*. 98th Congress, 2d session, 1984.

U.S. Congress. Senate. *Senate Report 98-425*. 98th Congress, 2d session, 1984.

U.S. Council for International Business. *A New MTN: Priorities for Intellectual Property*. New York, 1985.

Vaitsos, C. V. "Patents Revisited: Their Function in Developing Countries." *Journal of Development Studies* (October 1972).

Vernon, Raymond. *The International Patent System and Foreign Policy*. Study no. 5, U.S. Congress, Senate, Judiciary Committee, Subcommittee on Patents, Trademarks, and Copyrights. Washington, D.C., 1957.

Webster, David. "Direct Broadcast Satellites: Proximity, Sovereignty, and National Identity." *Foreign Affairs* (Summer 1984).

"Who Owns the Idea?" *Omni* (March 1985).

"Why Investors Are Losing Their Biotechnology Bug." *Economist*, December 8, 1984.

Williams, Sidney B. "Protection of Plant Varieties and Parts as Intellectual Property." *Science* 225, July 6, 1984.

World Intellectual Property Organization. *General Information*. Geneva, 1984.

DATE DUE